The POWER of CATS For Kids

HuaYi Wei

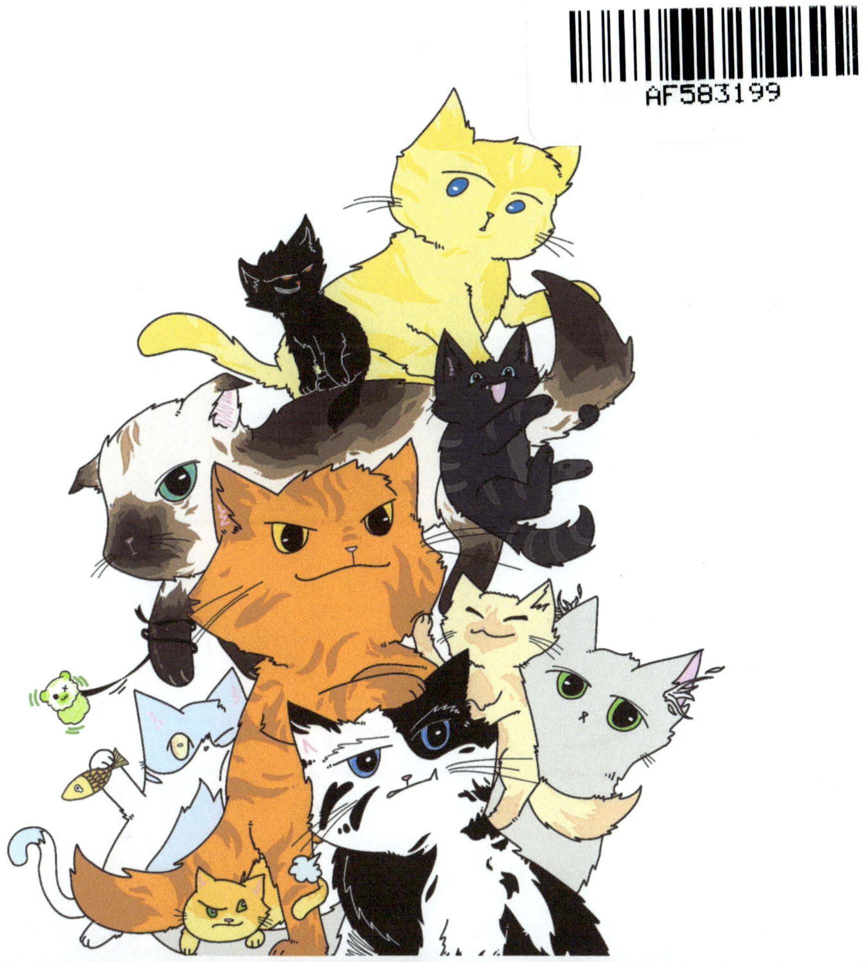

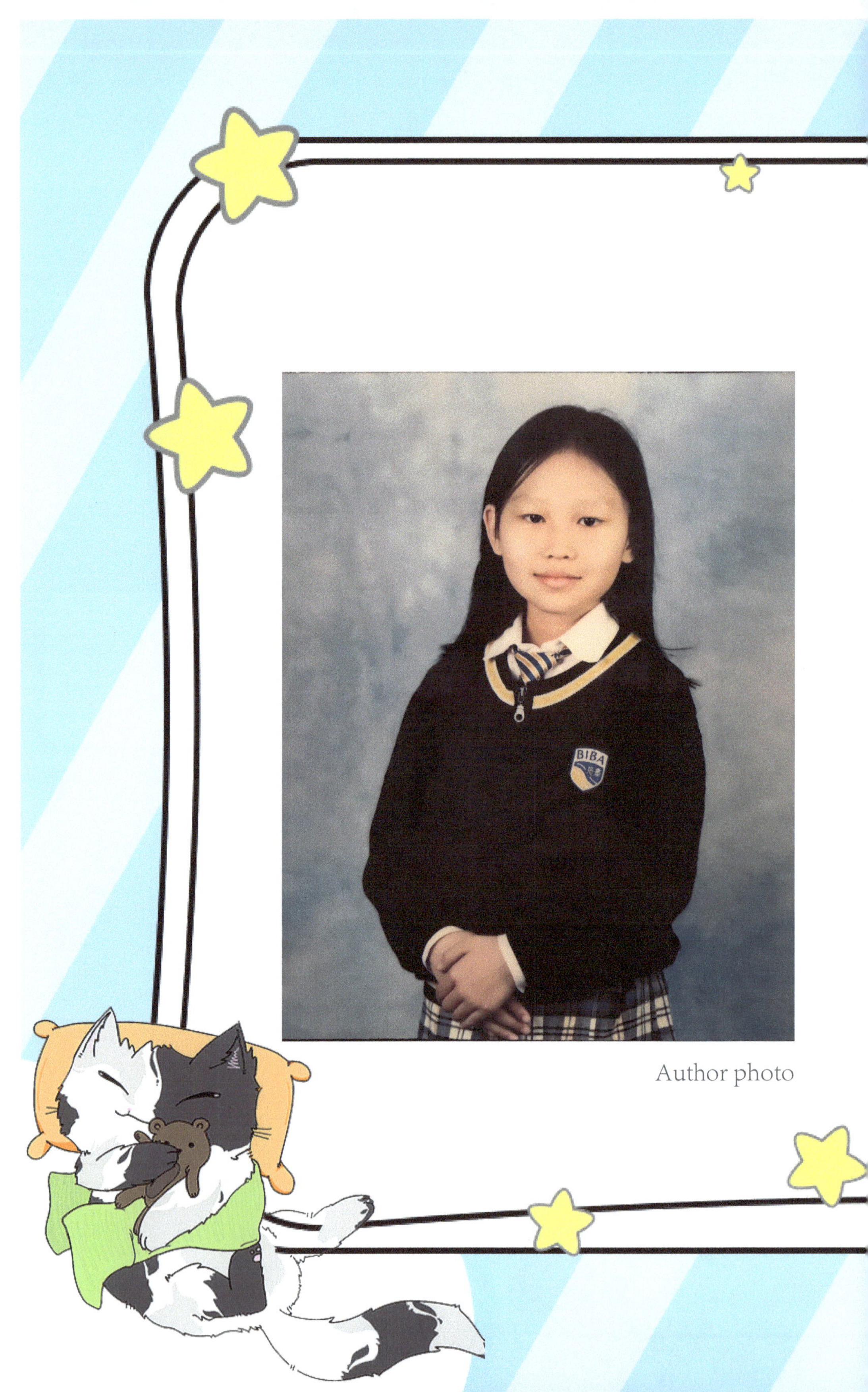

Author photo

HuaYi Wei is a 11 years old girl who has had a passion for writing and drawing cats since she was a baby. As a cat lover, Huayi's love for her cat Viva inspired her to write "The Power of CATS." She wrote this book when she was 9 years old, and she did more than 60 drawings of cats in collaboration with her father, Hai Wei, an illustration artist. As a middle school student now, she never stops creating stories and paintings. This is her first book ever published, but it will not be the last. Huayi currently lives in New York city with her family, and her cat Viva.

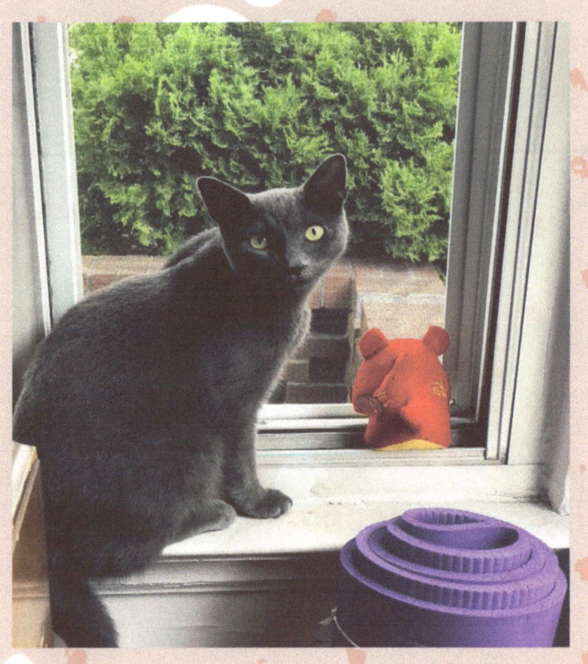

Viva

This book is for my very own cats——Viva, Xiao Mi, and Tao, with love and thanks.

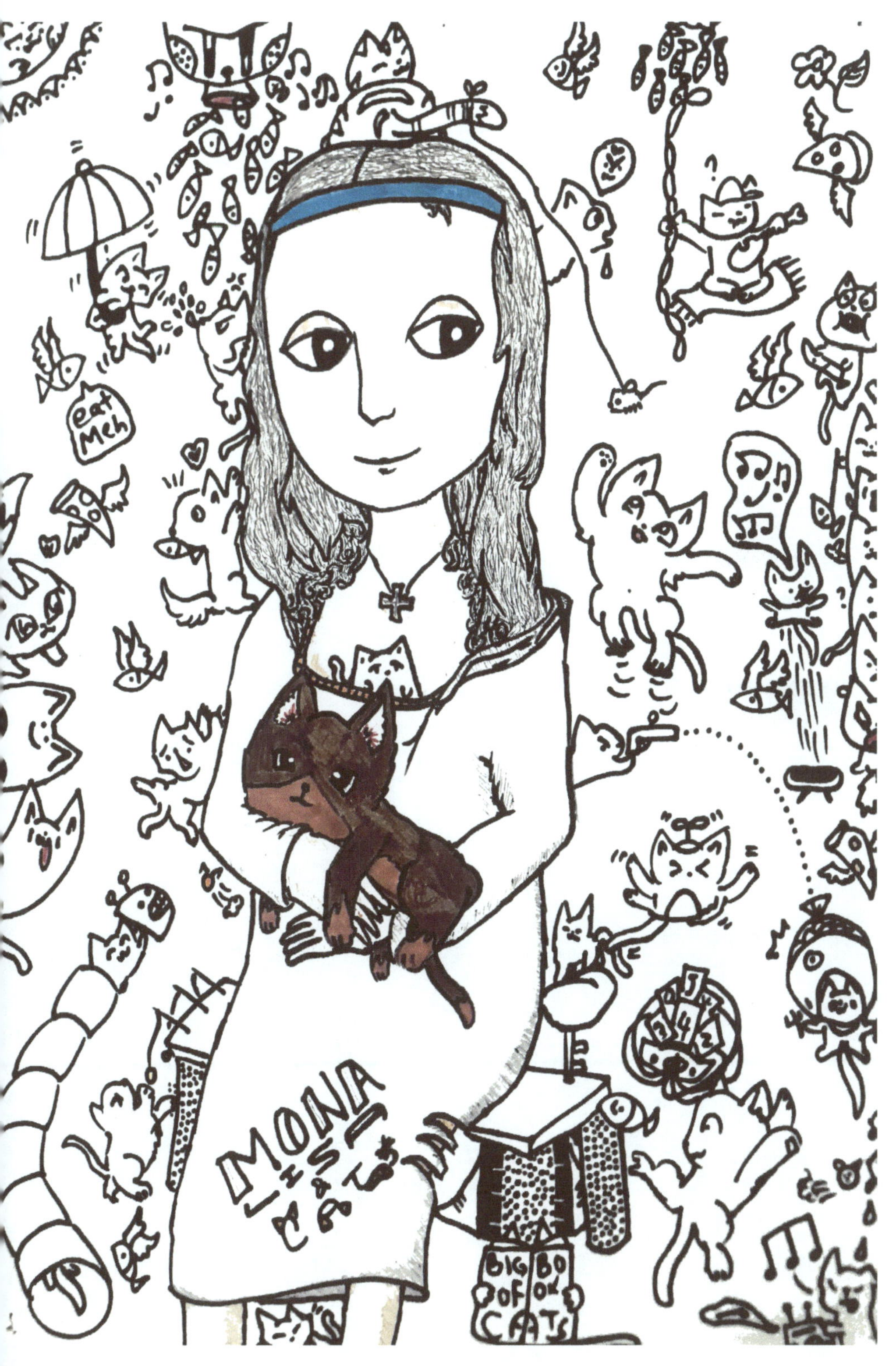
eat Meh
MONA LISA & CAT
BIG BOOK OF CATS

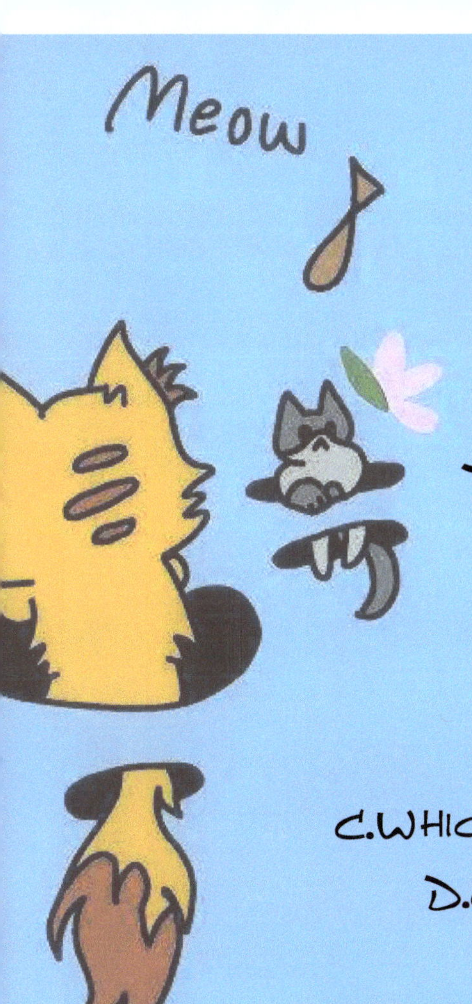

Meow

TABLE OF CATS

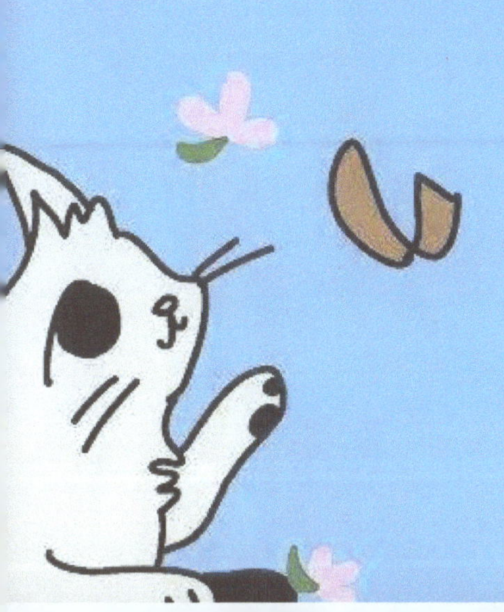

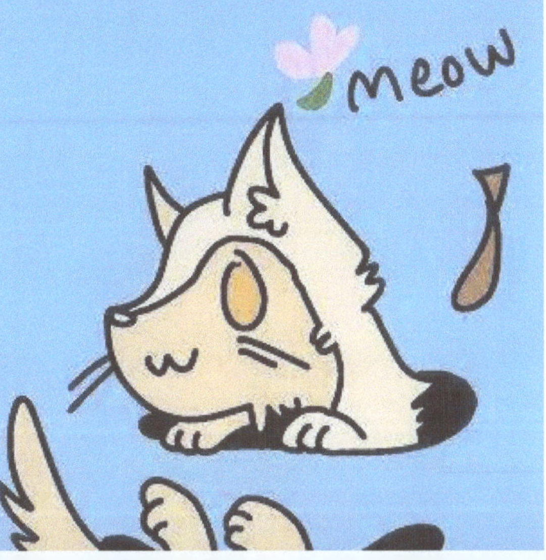

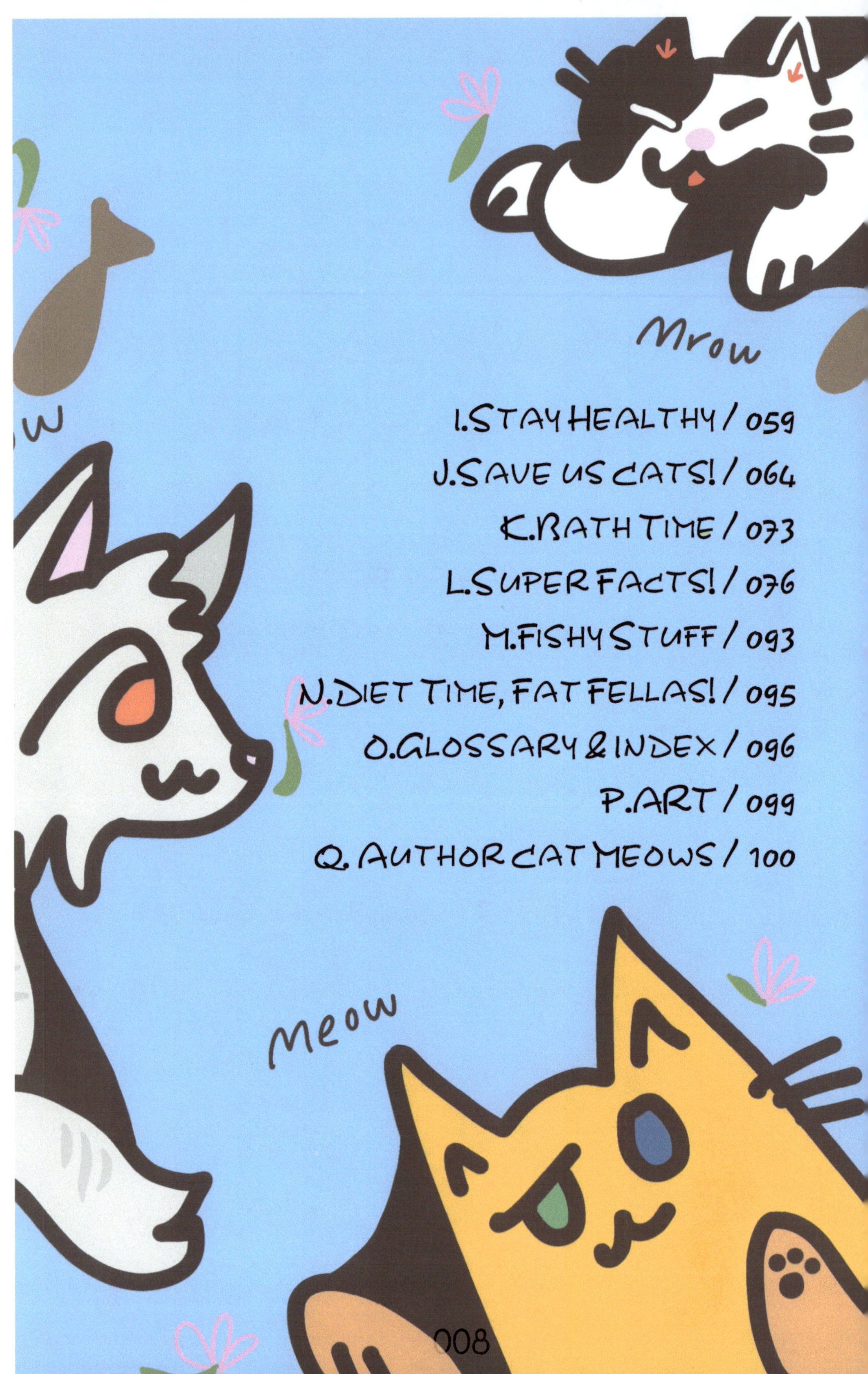
Mrow
Meow

Attention: Some stuff written here are my opinions

Our three little narrators (Tao, Viva, and Mi)

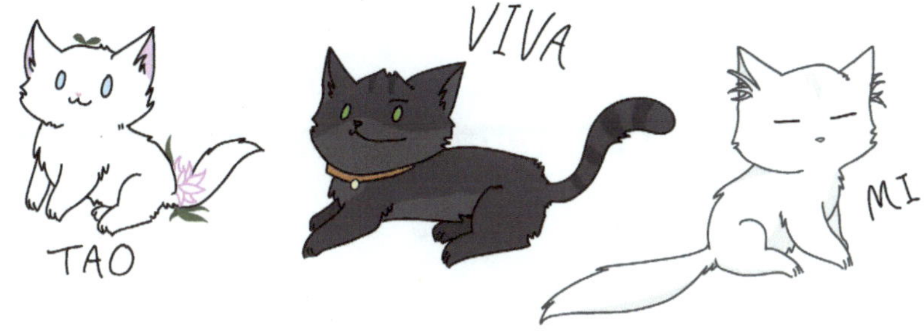

Intro-Cats

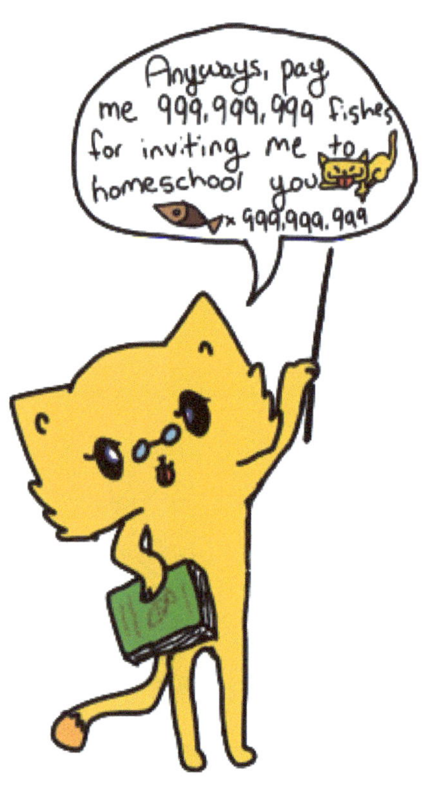

What has pointy ears, fluffy fur, shiny eyes, and a long, delicate tail? You guessed it, a cat! Our names, depending on this book AND in real life, are Tao, Mi, and Viva——the cat siblings! But do you know all about us? *Imagine being the only creature on Earth that purrs, sleeps an average of 16 hours a day, and uses 75% of their waking time cleaning*

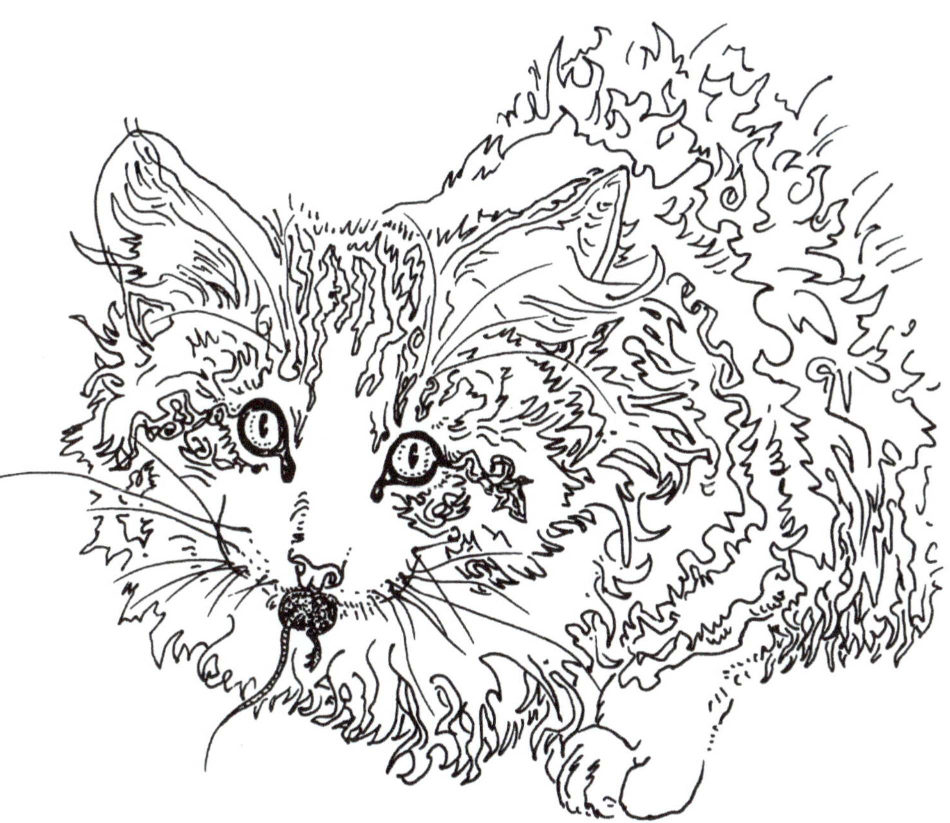

themselves.

(Tao: "I am a cat. And us cats are complicatedly cute.")

Well, if you do, I just wanna say cats are not only cute. (Mi: "Meow, lemme speak") Every question is supposed to have an answer, but with cats, you never know. (Tao: "Don't you agree?") For example, scientists never found out why cats purr. Some things

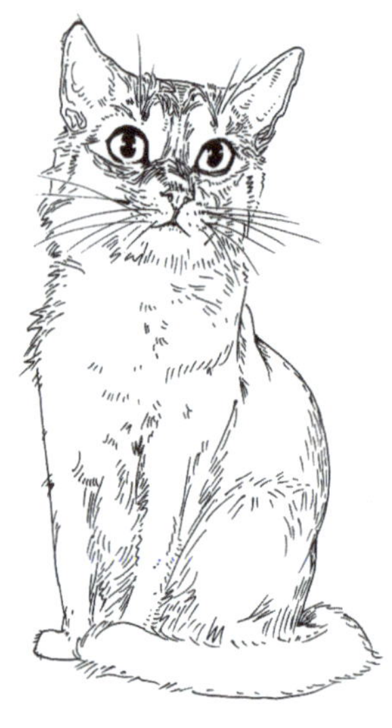

we take in are the closest and latest predictions about real life. Cats are like any other creatures in the world... one with their own backstory and appearance... But if there is one thing we are certain about, it's that we're all living in the same world. (Viva: YESH.) Actually, us cats can be a human's best friend, too, like the dog next door. If you just give us a chance to show that we are not mindless creatures... I mean, do you know who

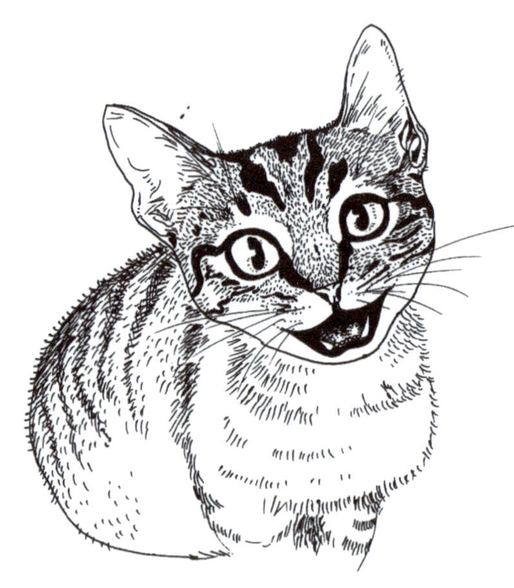

we really are!? If you want to know us more BEFORE YOU SET DOWN COMMENTS, then I guess it's time to start learning about us first. There are more than 50 kinds of domestic cats (look below), or more facts and proof of cats' appearances. You know, this book is not just some cheesy cat book...

TAKING CARE OF A CAT IS HARD WORK! THINK BEFORE YOU EVER ADOPT A CAT! HERE ARE SOME CHOICES

Domestic Cat Kinds;

✓Abyssinian

✓LaPerm

✓American Bobtail

✓Maine Coon

✓American Curl

✓Manx

✓ American Shorthair
✓ Munchkin
✓ American Wirehair
✓ Nebelung
✓ Angora
✓ Norwegian Forest Cat
✓ Australian Mist
✓ Ocicat
✓ Balinese
✓ Oriental
✓ Bengal
✓ Persian
✓ Birman
✓ Peterbald
✓ Bombay
✓ Pixiebob
✓ British Longhair
✓ Ragamuffin

✓ British Shorthair
✓ Ragdoll
✓ Burmilla
✓ Savannah
✓ California Spangled
✓ Scottish Fold
✓ Chartreux
✓ Selkirk Rex
✓ Chausie
✓ Serengeti
✓ Cornish Rex
✓ Siamese
✓ Cymric
✓ Siberian
✓ Devon Rex
✓ Singapura
✓ Egyptian Mau
✓ Snowshoe

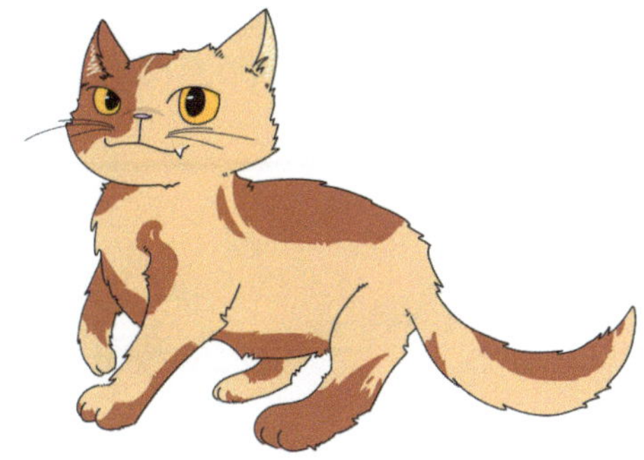

- ✓ European Shorthair
- ✓ Sokoko
- ✓ Exotic Shorthair
- ✓ Somali
- ✓ Havana Brown
- ✓ Sphynx
- ✓ Highlander
- ✓ Tonkinese
- ✓ Japanese Bobtail
- ✓ Toyger
- ✓ Korat

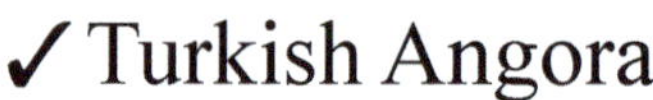

- ✓ Turkish Angora
- ✓ Kurilian Bobtail
- ✓ Turkish Van
- ✓ Lambkin

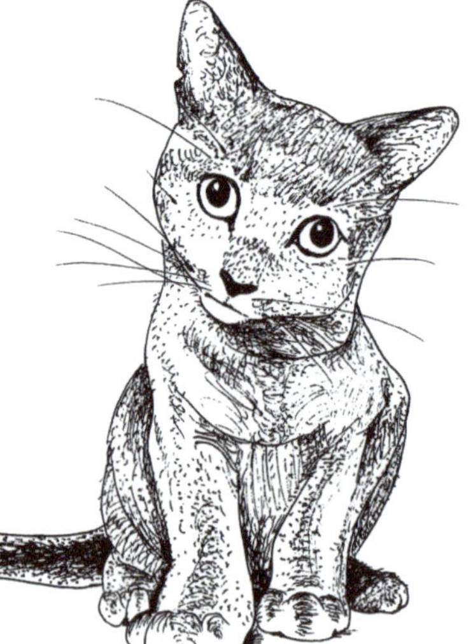

My First Cat!

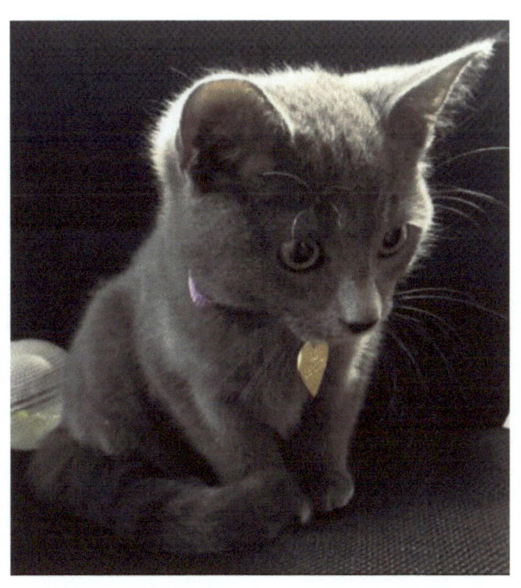

Adopting a cat = EASY; Taking care of a cat = HARD

Below are some theories about cats that may or may not be true... along with comments by Mi and Tao

-All it takes to adopt a cat is go to a pet store and gather supplies, then go to an animal adoption place or pet clinic, find the cat you adore, and then sign some paperworks to bring it home. WRONG! Or technically right. Do you think it is that easy to care for a pet, especially a cat?! Before you do those things, make sure you know what you are doing and receive permission from your family JUST IN CASE. You have to make your house pet-friendly... love the cat with all your heart… (Tao: "There could be stray cats in the streets too... I'd suggest giving it some food and bringing it to an animal hospital for a check up and afterwards, an animal shelter to give it a place to live. If you decide to adopt it, go ahead. Please, this saves lives.")

-Cats are usually shy of strangers and take a while to get used to people. However, beware, cats are not as "easy" as they look... in fact, taking care of them could be a racket! Make sure you are not allergic, have your house fully prepared, and are willing to sac-

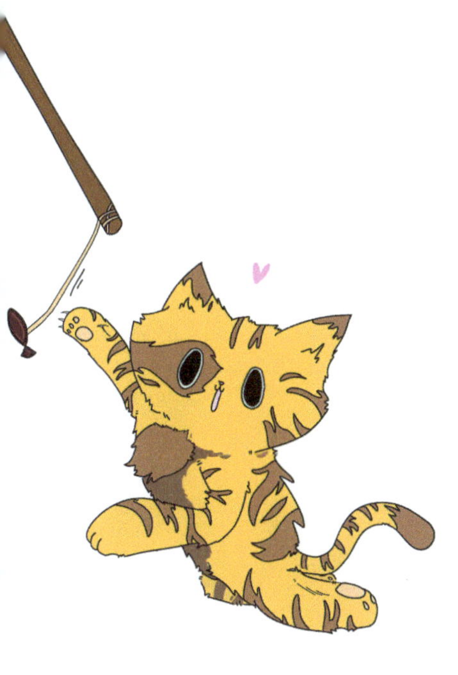

rifice a few pieces of furniture and money, let alone time, for this kitty. Right! But still, like all other creatures on Earth, cats have different personalities so what is said here may not always be right. You have to observe your cat's actions and figure out a way around it, even if it means throwing this book in the trash. (Tao: "You'll have to be prepared to handle everything from us cats, and think first before you decide to adopt any one of us... Look in "Fishy Stuff" for more information.")

-Your cat is more than just a pet, in fact, they're more like a 2-year-old child (who thinks like one), which makes them your re-

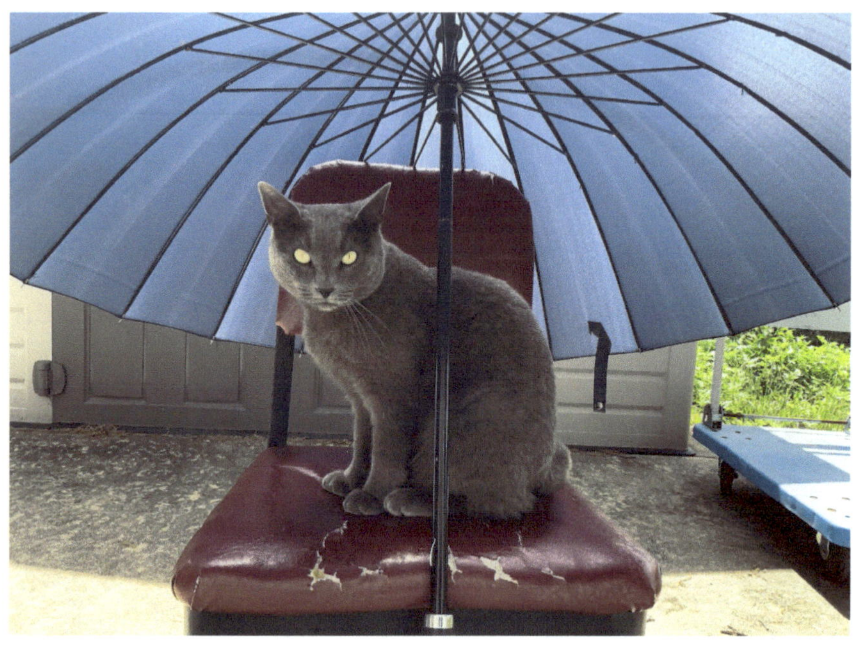

sponsibility. Everything needed for the cat is necessary. Think; your cat, your family member/ best friend! YES! (Mi: "Get up when your cat needs your help, that's why you adopted him in the first place. Clean his litter box, play with him, protect and feed him, and treat him as a trouble-making family member! Remember, think before you do something small, since small things can lead to huge consequences) Once you make your decision to adopt a cat, it's done. The cat is now your responsibility and you are going to keep him forever unless you MUST let go. But we are going to do the best that we can give to our new family member, right?

-Cats are intelligent animals that can understand certain things we say (such as "Time to eat!" and their names). They get used to something, and they live that way. Depends. Like I said, it really depends on the cat, its adapting skills, and the environment. It might take longer for older, wiser cats to get used to a new place since they used to live in a different lifestyle. If the environment is big and full of strange smells and things, they might also take longer to get used to.

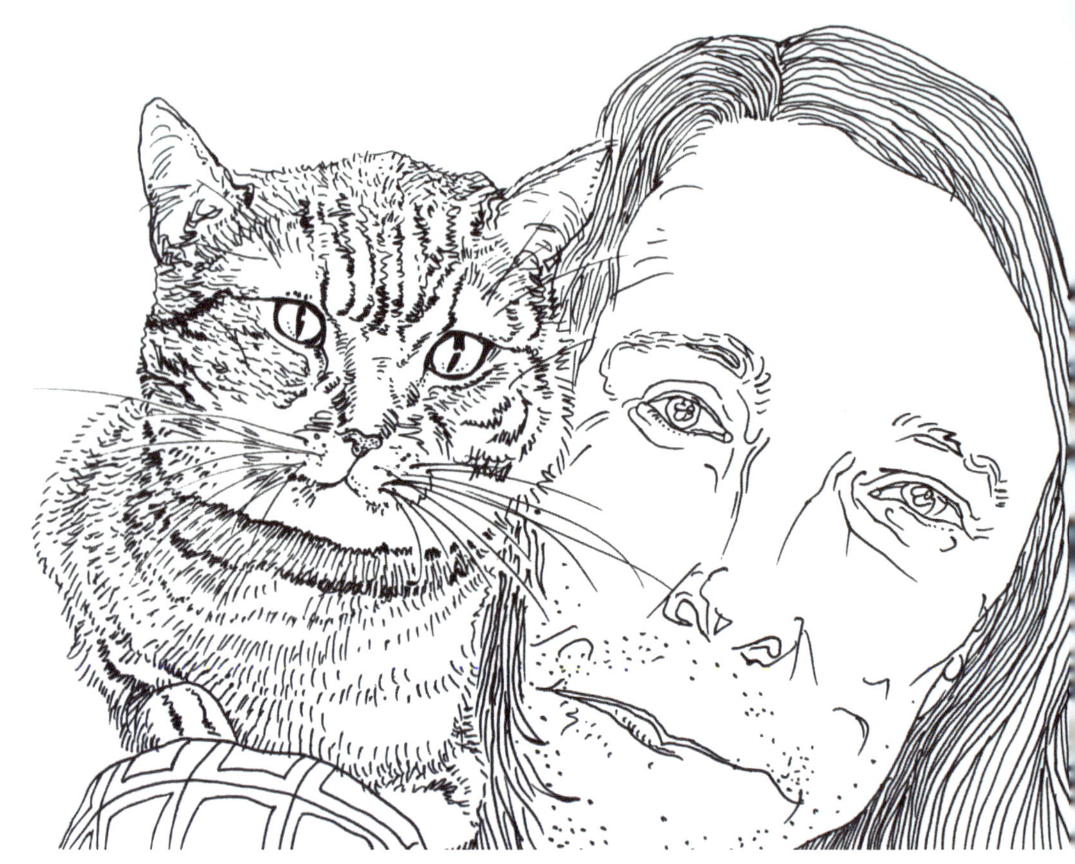

Which Cat are YOU?

Read to find out which one of these awesome Top10 Cats have your traits!

American Shorthair-

Traits- It has ALL of the traits, plus, they even have more than 80 colors.

Bengal-

Traits- Always flaring up like flame, active, curious, loving, alert, and cunning at the same time.

Himalayan

Traits- Sweet, quiet, calm in many ways, always succeeds in finding a way of suiting itself and winning.

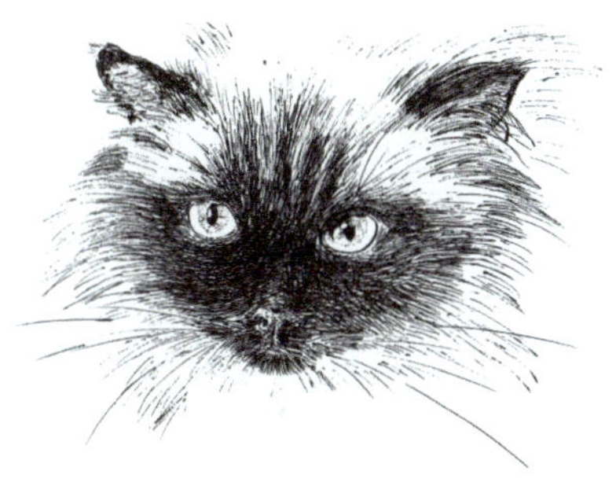

Maine Coon-

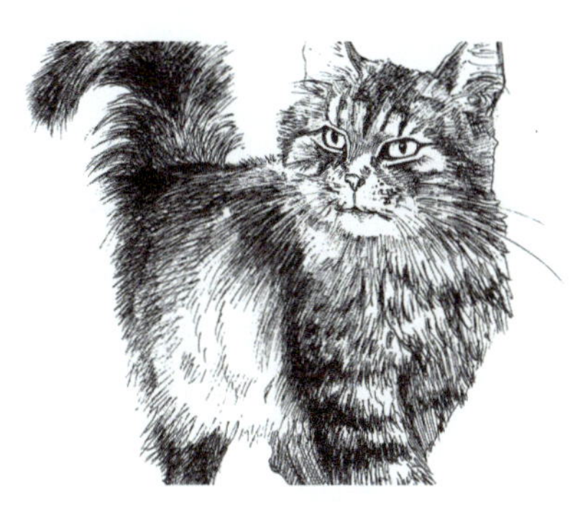

Traits- Dog-like, obedient, vigorous + tough on the outside but actually friendly and sweet. Affectionate yet goofy.

Manx-

Traits- 1% aggressive, 99% attached to humans, small, social, shy, playful, a tiny bit dog-like (some can fetch small items!)— quite intelligent, as you can see.

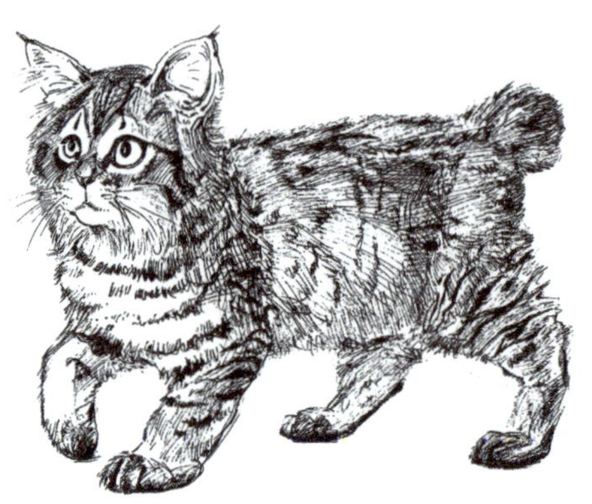

Persian-

Traits- Quiet yet affectionate, punchy-faced, sweet, easygoing, easily annoyed; (False Fact: "I'm not fat!" Excuses: "it's just the fur...")

Ragdoll-

Traits- Amazing mood, loyal, gentle, sociable, a born champion yet affectionate towards humans!

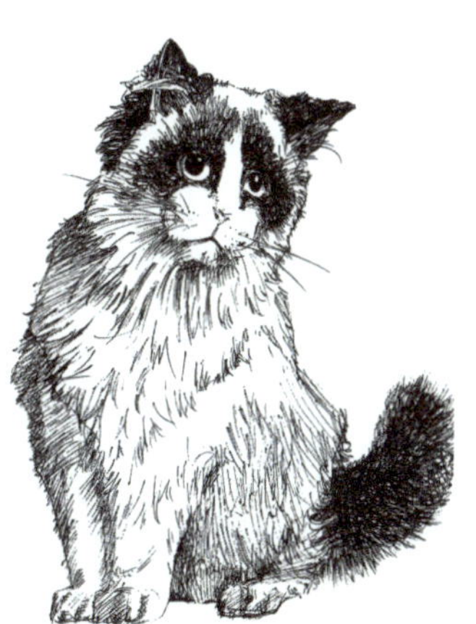

Russian Blue-

Traits- Quiet, shy, calm, smart, curious, loving, playful, sensitive to human feelings, and attached to only their owner(s).

Siamese-

Traits- Loyal, energetic, playful, affectionate, curious, intelligent, and 100% clean.

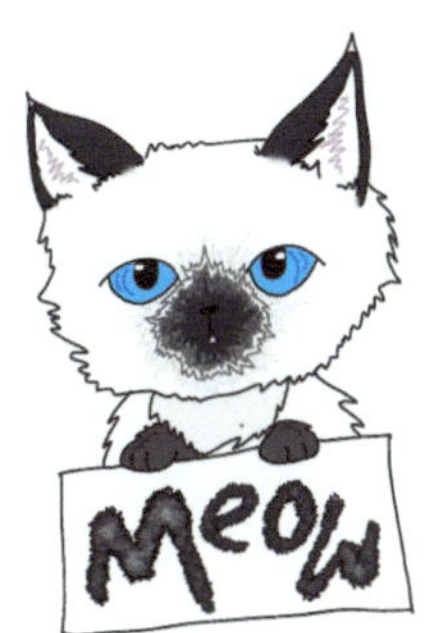

Sphynx-

Traits- "PURRRRR!" This intelligent, friendly, social, attention-seeking, inquisitive (meaning: curious), hairless, and gentle cat is really affectionate towards humans.

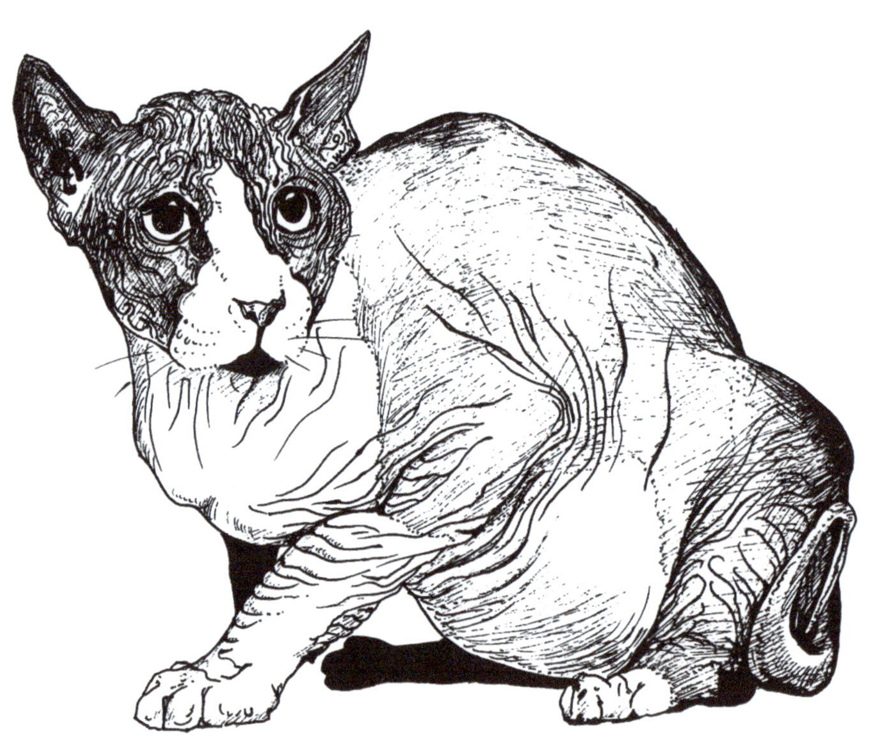

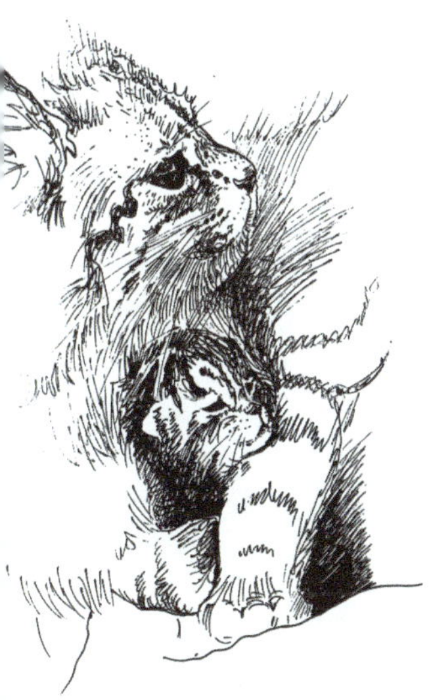

Cat Dictionary

Purr- When a cat purrs, she is feeling comfortable and safe

Meow- Cats' meows can mean anything ("Feed meeeeeeeeee").

Hiss- A cat's warning when it is in a uncomfortable, fearful, or stressful mood

Growl- Growling or spitting happens when a cat feels either annoyed, frightened, or angry.

Yowl- A yowl can mean a lot of things; scared, looking for a mate, in pain, or accomplished.

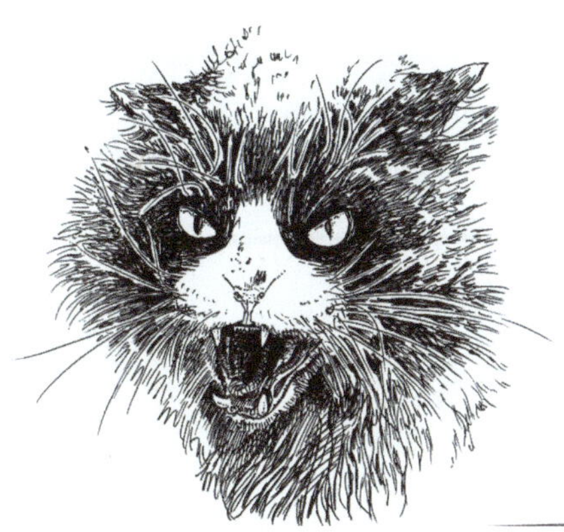

Windy Nights

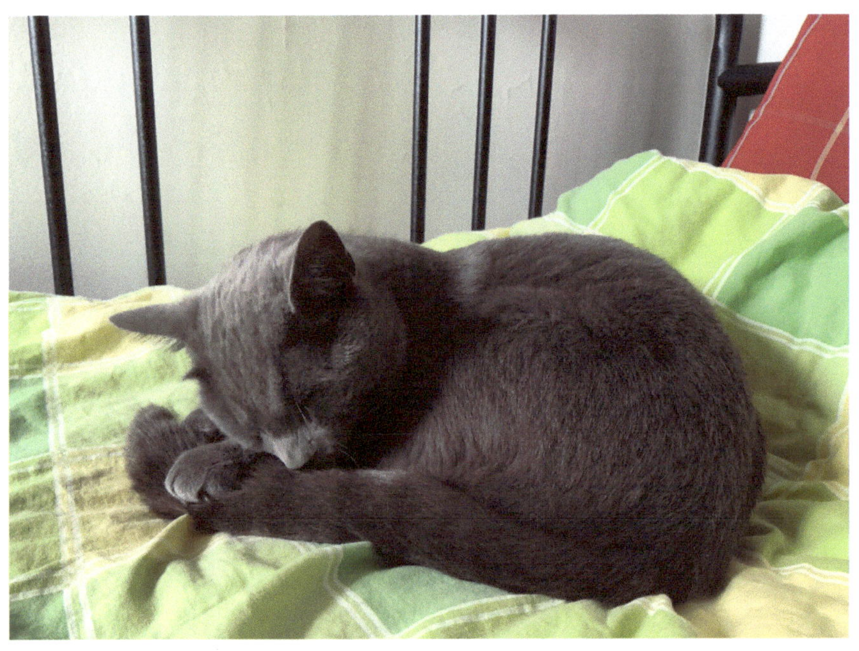

Neither moves. Neither meows. Neither- "Stop chewing on my shoes!" On windy nights, when everyone is sound asleep, us cats are busy doing something else! Cats are often playful at night and lazy in the daytime (According to the cat instincts, it is usually nighttime when cats hunt). A pair of eyes that shine in the dark can help the cat see better in the dim light! Those wonderful shiny eyes can only work in the dim light. And as you can see, your cat can move her ears from side to side to hear the quietest sound with 33 muscles! You might get worried if your cat sees danger at night, but you don't need to be. 'Cause your cat has a pair of shiny eyes, strong sharp teeth, tuna breath, and, of course, deadly claws! (IT'S FOR ME TO KNOW AND YOU TO FIND OUT, FELLAS.) This is more than enough to be safe all the time, even when the cat is alone, plus whenever your cat feels threatened, she also has run-away feet to run away from danger. Everything your cat does is just a cat's instincts, or a cat's normal behavior.

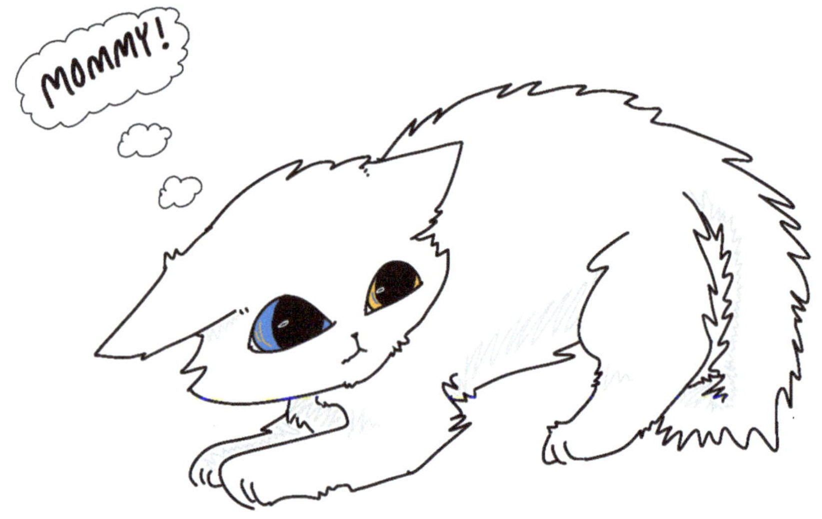

Don't get scared if you see those crazy-shiny-eyes, it is a clue to find the hidden cat in the dark! Every cat has the 'eye power' to see in the dark as midnight hunters... but don't forget the felidae! This ameow-zing and pawsome cat family consists of mammals of all sizes including tigers, lions, leopards, cheetahs, cougars, lynxes, ocelots, and, of course, domestic cats .

Domestic cats are the smallest members

in the felidae. Lions and tigers are the biggest, and they, too, have good eyesights. Nighttime or not, their instincts benefit them in many ways. Do not stare at your a cat's shinny eyes, they might find it uncomfortable and weird. When a cat's got complicated feelings,

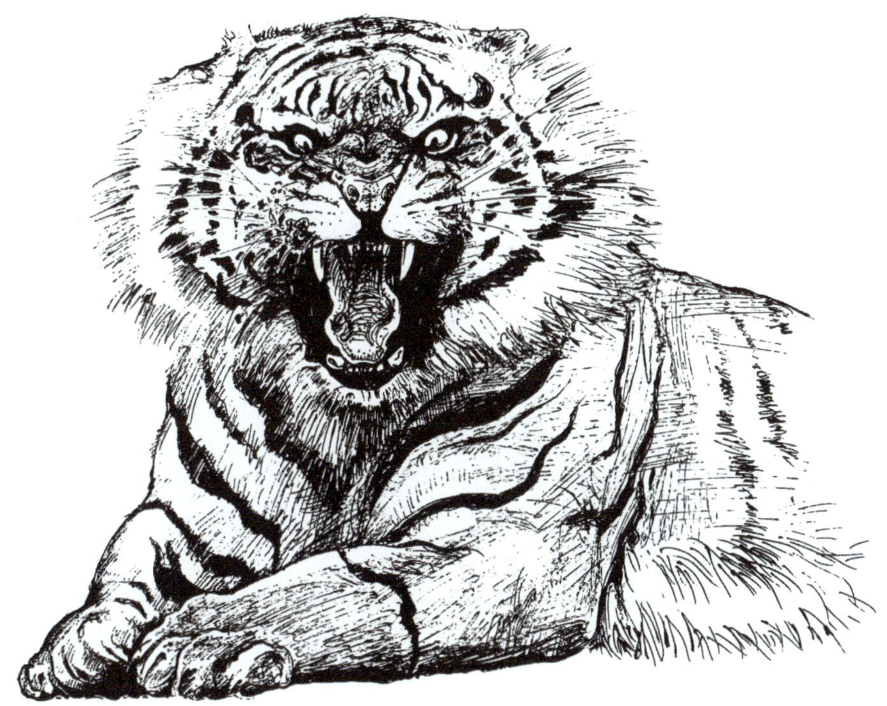

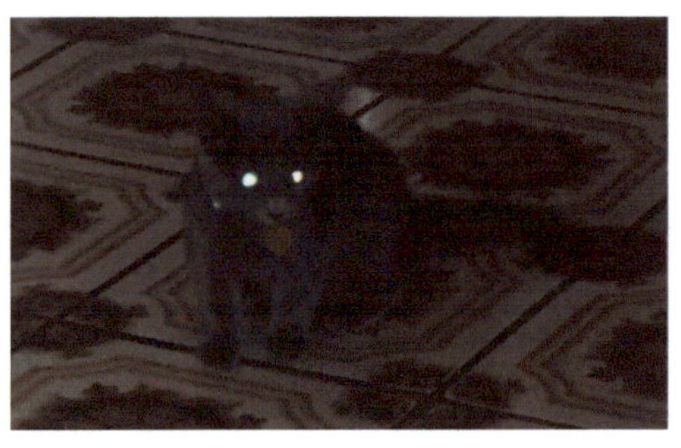

the "tiger power" will be borrowed and you will be sorry. (WATCHING OUT is for your OWN SAFETY!) You mayyyy find your cat sleeping during daytime and watchingggggg you during nighttime... just remember, you might wake up one day and find your house a mess, with a mouse tail hanging from your cat's mouth, more or less! A startled sleeping cat is not good, either, because even though sometimes your cat may look sound asleep, its senses are still very strong and active...

Kittens All Around

CAT AGES (MEOW-CTIONARY)

Kitten (baby): birth to 6 months / Young cat (junior): 6 months to 2 years / Cat (adult): 3 to 6 years / Matured (wise cats): 7 to 10 years / Senior (old wise cats): 11 to 14 / Super Senior (VERY old wise cat): 15 and up

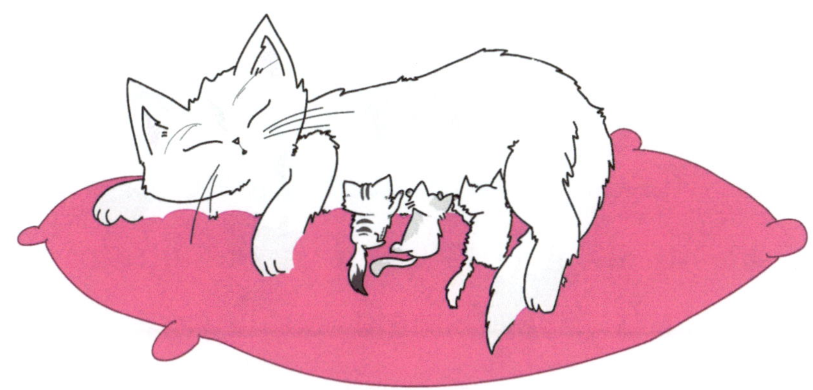

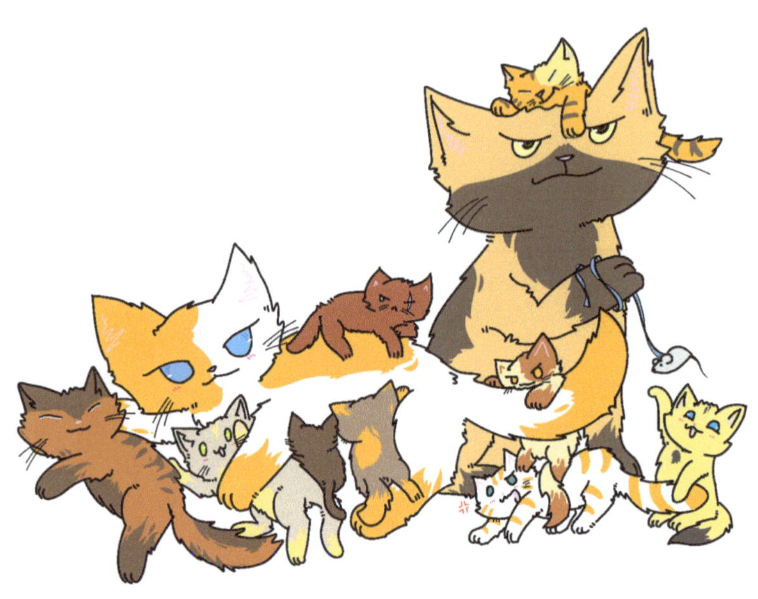

Milk drinkers, momma's babies, small crawlers… Kittens! Look how cute they are, aww... But you can't just stand there and do nothing! If you want to help the mama cat from being in too much stress, you better help her. Starting from giving her a LOTTA healthy food for energy and help her carry her kittens, if she lets you. However, ignore the cat instincts. Every single mama cat loves its babies; and they sometimes overprotect them. Well... A momma cat does lots of hard work for her babies. If she ignores the work (which she doesn't), about 2-13 kittens that are born in the litter are not going to be as healthy. Still, cats mature quickly. When human babies are 12-18 months old, they are busy learning to walk while the cats are already full-grown. However, don't separate kittens from their mothers before that, or they will have trouble learning basic stuff, like how to use the litter box, how to hunt and play, and how to eat solid food… Momma cats feed their babies milk for nutrition, just like us, for we are all mammals (They continue this action until they grow independent after about 2 months). For the worst, some kittens are going to... well, die. The kittens NEED their mother, or anyone close to a mother, before they are ready. That reminds me, mother cats can have unlimited amounts of litters in a lifetime. Although you could bring the cat to the pet hospital (not that she is sick or anything) to stop this action — but that would be cruel. The average lifespan of a cat is 13 — 14 years old, which is older than 75 years old in human years. The kittens need to stay with their guardians until they are at least 8 weeks old. If the kittens leave their mama younger than at least 2 months old, the kittens may not stay as healthy and knowledgeable because they need their mother's milk and her to teach them the basic cat knowledge. The kitten's fur colors are based on its ancestors, or elder family members that could have passed away. The mothers will do everything and give anything to keep their kittens healthy. Sometimes the kitten's guardians, or parents will be dangerous, or even deadly to keep its kits from any danger, sometimes including its owners. For example, when cougars give birth to cubs, they lick the newborns over and over again in case a predator or enemy smells the kits and attacks them. Although there are no predators attacking domestic cats, they lick the kittens anyways to stay clean because

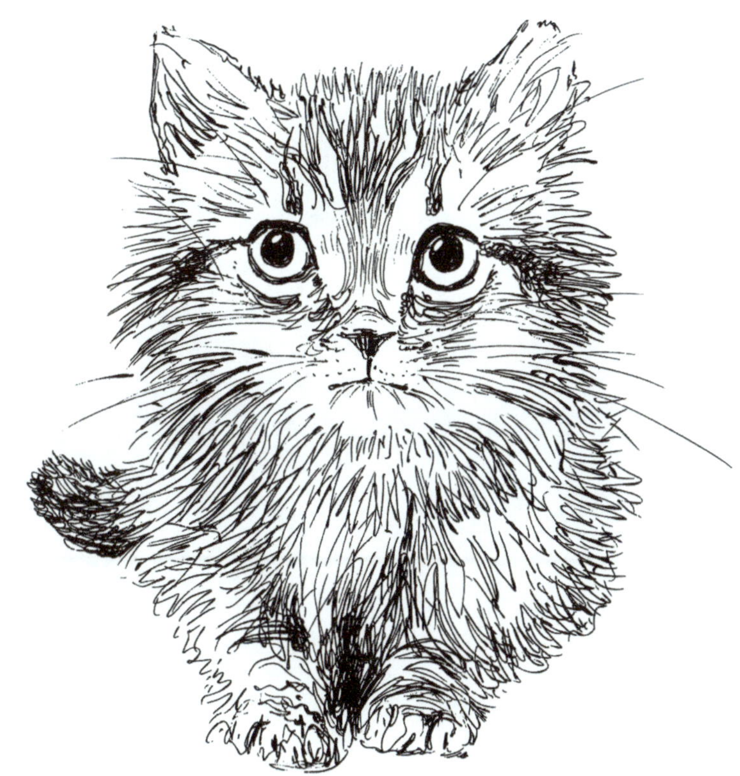

of, well, instincts. Cats are basically a smaller version of cougars. The mother always give the best to the kittens if she can, but, sadly (according to us), some female cats (mothers) would "shoo" the male cat (father) away, because they know better than keeping ANY danger near its babie. The mother can't even trust the father of their own kittens since the mom will sometimes be afraid if the father hurts her kittens, accidental or not. See, 'trust no one'. No matter how uneasy things are, the mother cares for her kittens and keeps them away from danger, even if it involves violence. Still, the momma felt grateful because she got a lot of little kits for her rewards of all the hard work she sacrificed. Kittens drink their mama's milk since birth, they look like their parents, breathe air with lungs, and have

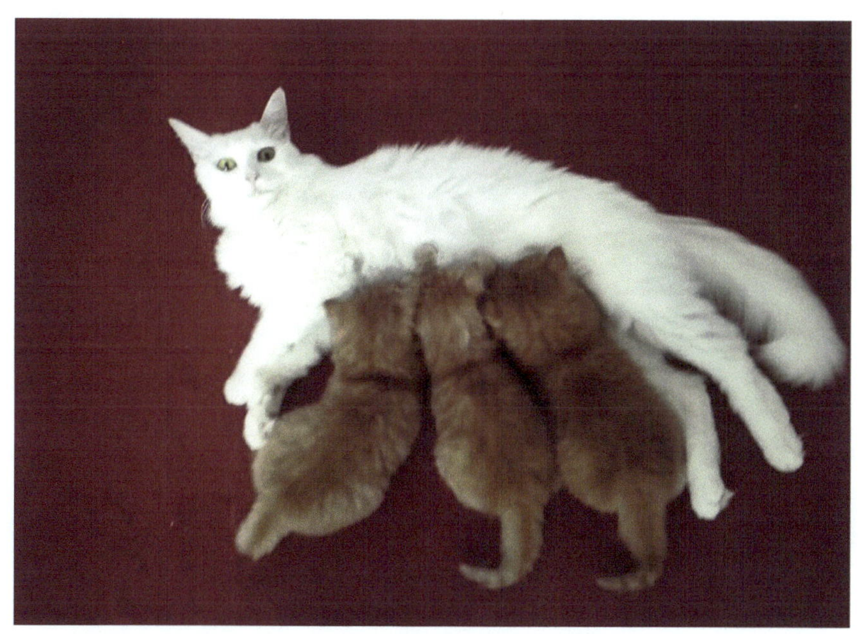

fur, this is why cats are mammals.

Strange, why do all kittens have blue eyes when their parents have different eye colors? All kittens are born with blue eyes since there is still liquid in the kitten's eyes. They open their eyes when they are about 2 weeks old, and… in about 8 weeks, the blue eye color changes into another eye color like its parents since the liquid is no longer there. The momma cat is going to be VERY tired when she take care of the babies! This is when... you chime in! You can help the mother cat around the house (if she lets you) by doing things such as carrying the kittens to the mother, feeding the mother cat, playing with the kittens, keeping the kitten out of trouble + danger... However, there is no need to feed the kits or bathe them unless you have to. Mother takes

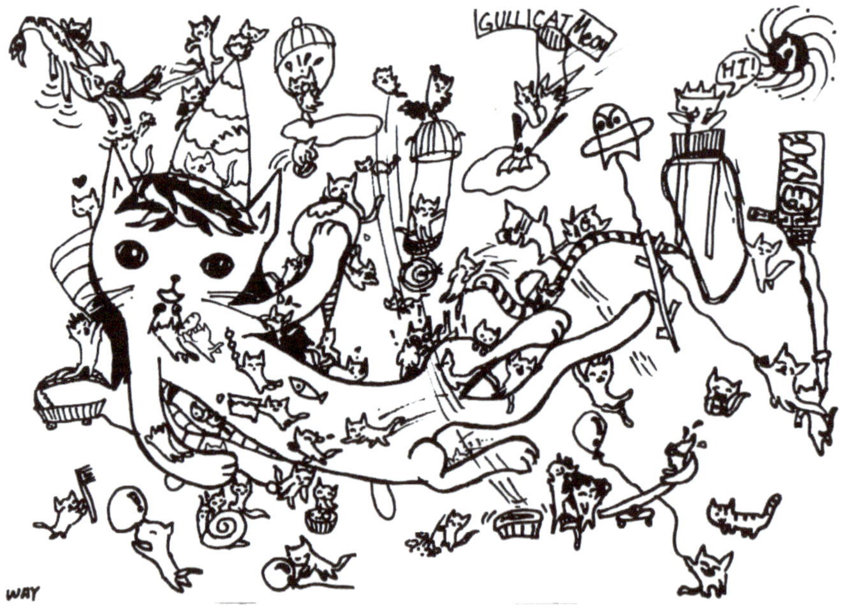

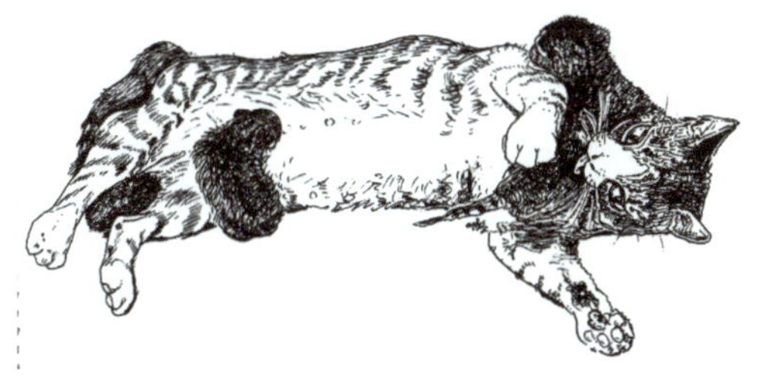

care of those things! Now it's time for you to bring the youngsters to play time! MEOW! It's finally time for the kittens to learn and play and be ready to grow into a young cat. The kittens are born predators like the rest of its family, remember that. It would be perfectly normal for a kitten to do some I-didn't-know-kittens-can-do-that kind of things. Kittens had great instinct just like their mother, but they don't have much self-control and knowledge yet. You will never be as great as the mother cat in taking care of her kittens, but what we do is enough. So, help the mama deal with the babies by looking at these paragraphs below!

SAY WHAT?! You Are The Vet!?
Mother + Newborn Kitten Guide

1. Settle your cat somewhere comfortable and safe; such as a blanket under a box

2.After a kitten "comes out," cut the Placenta (the sticky red thing on it's tummy button) off the newborn kitty, the cat giving birth will eat it for more energy. (Remember to wear gloves and be extra extra careful! Kittens are alway the smallest, most careless, and weakess...)

3.Wipe the cat with some tissues (on the place that is giving birth to kittens...) so the cat giving birth does not feel as disgusted or unsettled.

4.Pet the future mother more so she will feel a little more comfortable and for doing such a good job.

5.Give the mother goat milk for more energy.

6.Give your cat some space; having babies is personal!

7.IF: one of the kittens died, do not let the mother cat know. Like us, cats have feelings. Bury the kitten.

Kitty Time!
Playtime Guide

-No leaving mama-

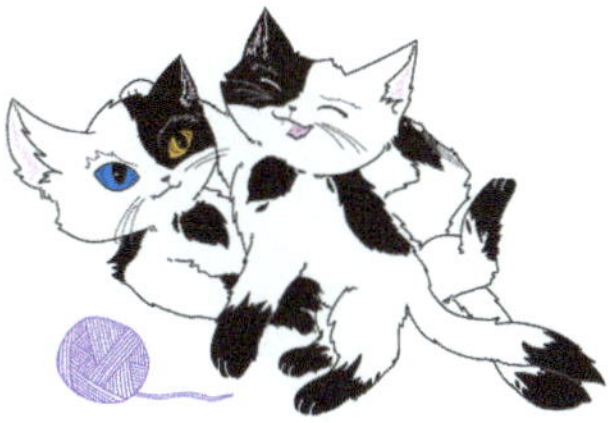

-Kittens can't be left alone-

-No small toys such as a piece of lego or string (kittens and even cats might swallow it by accident)-

-Don't let too much people see the kittens

since the kittens are weak and shy of strangers-

-Take care the troubles & play-

-OPTIONAL: Train the kitten with a cat toy or something the cat can't easily swallow. You can also teach it paw-shaking. If the kitten gets what you are doing, give the kitty treats as rewards. (kittens are easier to train, full-grown cats are harder)

-Be good monitors and take care of the kitties!

Weirdly True Cats

Mother cats cannot count, but she changes places she settles in often to raise her kittens whenever she feels insecure or threatened in that area. (Cat moms usually prefer a place that does not attract much attention; such as a box/under something) But... if the mother had too many kittens, she might leave a kitten behind when she is busy carrying other kittens to the new settlement. Help the cat and bring the kittens back to her (or to wherever she settled in)!

Cat Words

Kitten - A young cat that still needs care from its mother.

BABY KITTY TIMELINE STUFF

How long will the cat be pregnant for: 58-67 days.

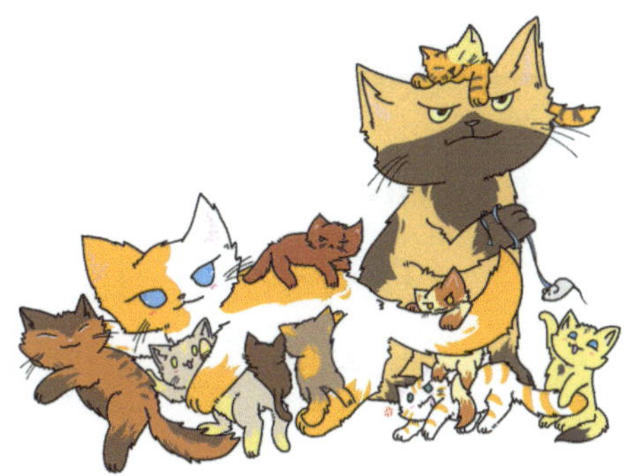

How many kittens in a litter: 1-12 kittens.

How many litters can a cat have in a lifetime: unlimited.

How long until the kitten opens its eyes: 1-2 weeks.

How long until kittens can be separated from their mother: 12-14 weeks.

How long until kittens are ready for adoption: 3-6 months, but only if the kitten is ok with cat skills.

How long until kittens start walking and using the litter box: 3-5 weeks.

How long until the kitten starts socializing and taking its first vaccines: 4-8 weeks.

How long until the kitten starts learning cat skills: 9-12 weeks, it depends whether they are ready or not.

How long until the kitten is ready for adoption: 3-6 months.

Jump!

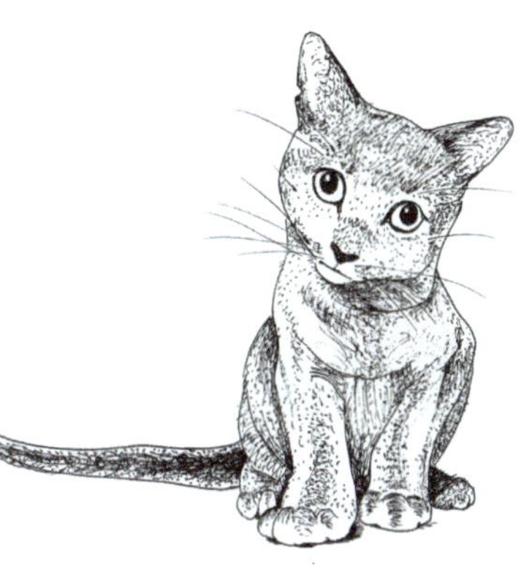

Wow! What a great jumper! How does a cat jump so high? Well, let's get straight to this question. First, a cat can- walk in straight lines, however that does not mean the cat will jump in straight lines! The power comes from the cat's legs and limbs, it depends on how hard the cat is trying and its strength to determine how powerful the jump is. A young, healthy, well-napped cat can jump 6 times its body length. Cats even use their tails to balance themselves! Jumping more will strengthen the cat's muscles, with practice it will benefit them in many ways. Still, no matter how high the jump is, the cat will land on their paws (feet). A cat can jump 8 feet and fall the same distance without hurting itself, afterall. An adult cat can jump up to 5 feet or more. However, it depends on how active the cat is, how old it is, how healthy it is, and how often it practices its "kitty powers." Eight weeks after a kitten is born, it starts moving (like, actually moving with a destination) and can jump an average of 1 feet or so, if it tries hard enough.

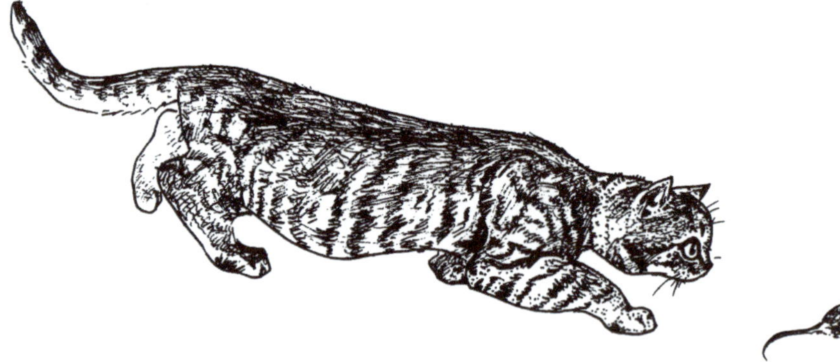

Food! A cat is getting hungry. The cat has the tiger power inside of them, remember? They are domestic animals, it doesn't mean they are not mousers, and doesn't have instinct! Instead of catching a deer, the predator cats would catch a mouse, and jumping and pouncing are required to do so. Some cats can even climb trees when they need to! These skills are still necessary for stray, hungry cats, unlike well-fed house cats. With practice, of course. Grabbing on to the tree with its claws, the cat is off and hunting a bird.

Cat Word

Predators- Animals that eat other animals.

Prey- An animal that could be hunted down and eaten by another animal.

HOW A CAT JUMPS UP

One, aim.

Two, kick its back legs to jump.

Three, balance.

Four, land on its front paws (pull itself up if nessecary).

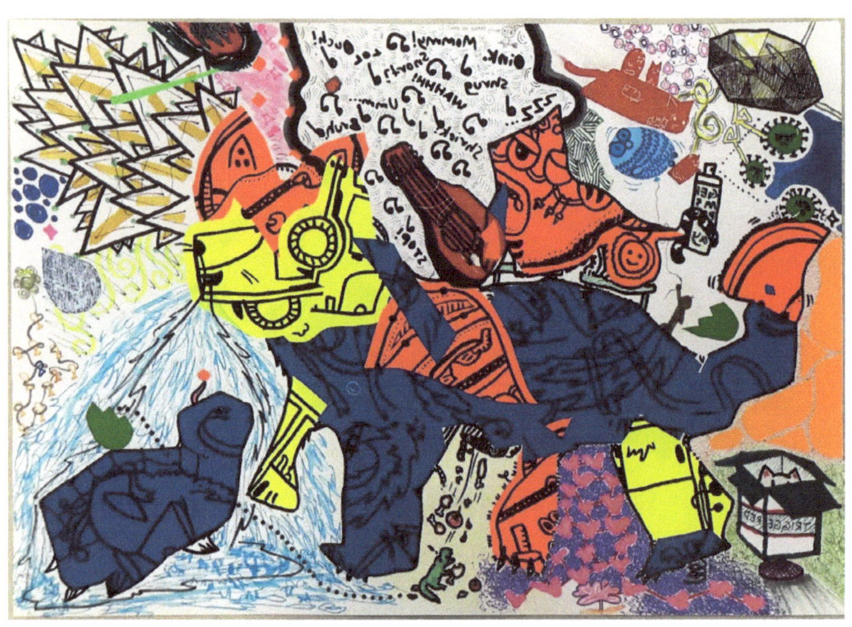

Try The NIRVANAS!

Beware of the cat nirvanas! Cats use their "kitty nirvanas" for many reasons. But, sometimes the kitty powers are a little TOO powerful and it backfires on them. Sometimes cats just want to play with you, but in a cat

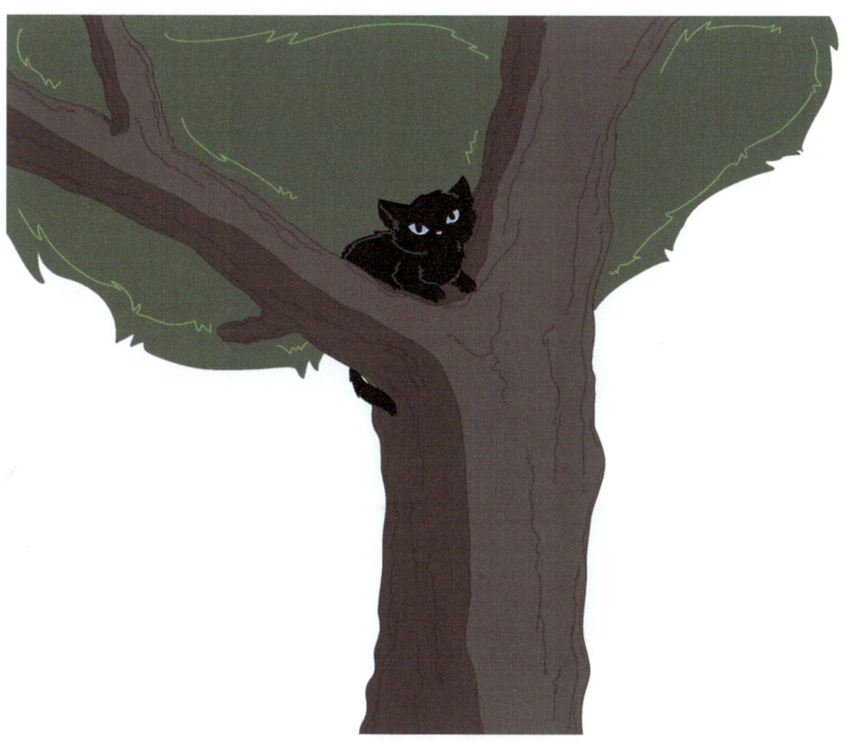

way, of course. Now, it's time to see if you can handle + understand your cat's tricks and survive...

ABILITY: STRONG HEARING

A cat's hearing ability can catch everything going on around it; with help from 33 muscles to catch every sound and movement, not even a mouse is able to steal and eat its cheese quietly... A cat's hearing can "pick up" sounds FIVE times farther than humans can...

Look at this picture above. Pretend: you are the poor little mouse that's "chosen" by the big grumpy cat. RUN!

ABILITY: SUPER EYESIGHT

All cats have "super eyesight" that can see in the dark, let alone glowing. It's eyesight can catch everything going on with just a glance; it also has eyeballs that can turn big and small depending on how the cats are feeling based on what they just caught with their

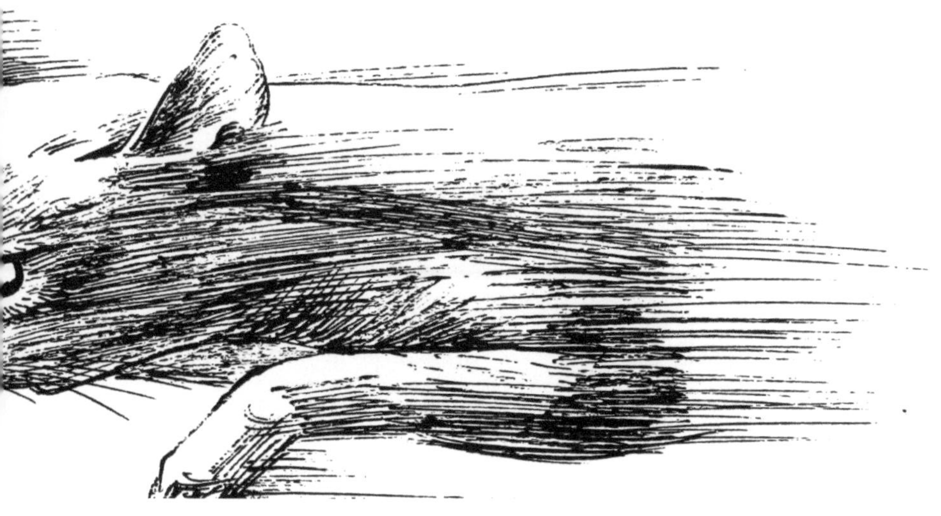

eyes. It can even be a movement of a mouse that can get a cat's feeling all mashed up into... excitement and enthusiasm.

ABILITY: DANGEROUS CLAWS

Watch out! Any wrong move in front of you cat will most likely make you suffer a cut from the claws; it's claws can not only scratch you, it is also a tool that can climb trees, scratch furniture, scratch other things, grow newer and even sharper nails (cut the nails once a week), pounce when needed, balance, run, defend itself from any danger, and most importantly, move around (like feet, but can do much

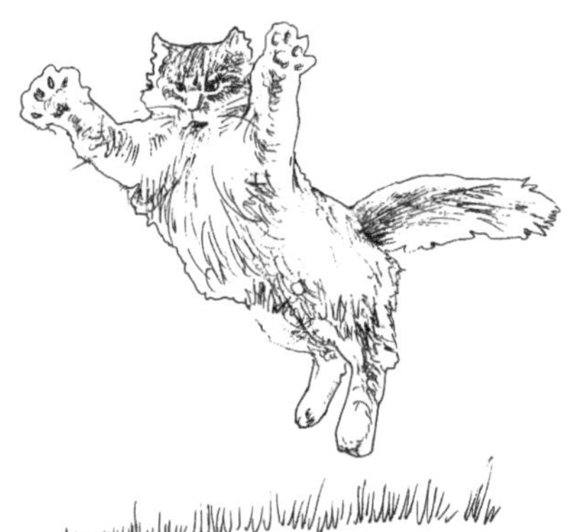

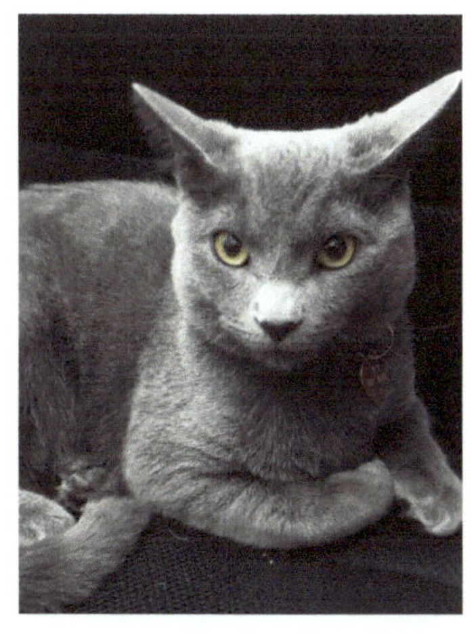

more!). However, do not declaw your cat to save trouble. Your cat may be troubled by many things it used to be able to do itself with instincts; the cat will be kicked out of the "cat circle" and it's as if it has a disability.

ABILITY: SUPER JUMP

All cats are amazing jumpers that can jump a maximum of 2.4 meters and land on their paws (almost always). Cats jump by kicking the ground with its back legs and land on its destination with all limbs; they can jump up to wherever they want as long as it's less than 2.4 meters high, since they might have trouble and can get hurt from the coming down. *Interesting fact: Cats are SUPER quiet when they are trying to catch prey to avoid being found... then they POUNCE!

ABILITY: RUNAWAY FEET

Whenever a cat senses danger or trouble, its runaway feet can get the cat out of the scene in no time. In fact, if the cat tries hard enough, they can run up to 30 miles per hour.

ABILITY: SENSIBLE WHISKERS

A cat's whiskers is like a sensor; it can determine the movement of things nearby without having to touch it, the airflow is enough. These whiskers also help cats measure tight spaces to decide whether they can fit through. Cats have a sensory organ at the end of their whiskers called a proprioceptor, which sends messages to the brain. If a cat has no whiskers, it often will become disoriented and have trouble moving around, even with instincts. A lost whisker will eventually grow back, yes, so the more whiskers they grow, the better.

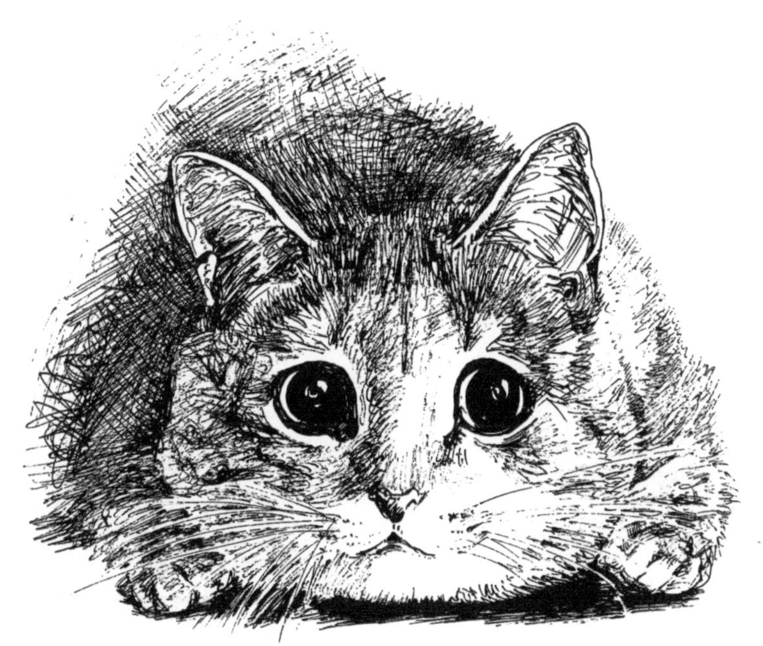

Sometimes, of course, the cats catch animals and play for fun (duh). Regular cats think like a two year old human, and they eat almost everything they catch or find, if their mood strikes them, sometimes, even when it is not edible. That's why you might see your cat bring home "supper," which will probably end up in the trash cans. A cat's prey might be mice, frogs, birds, bats, or lizards…

Fishy Word

Camouflage - surrounded by the background; hard to see.

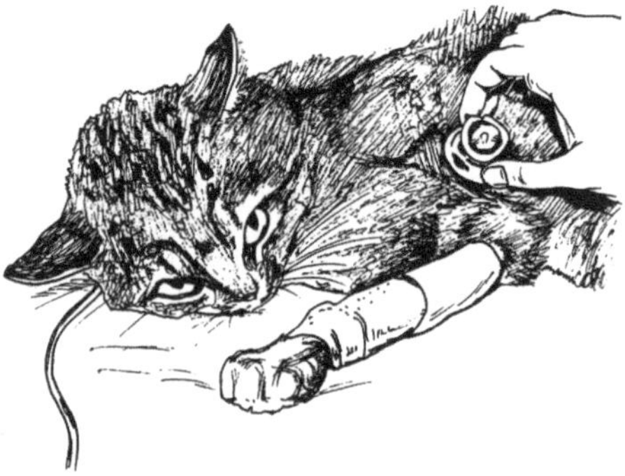

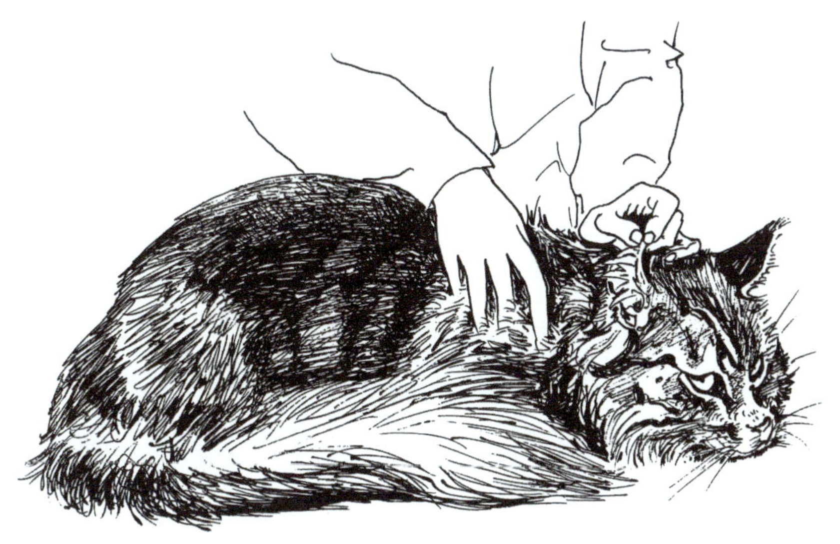

Stay Healthy

Why do we have vets? We need them for cats that are sick. But how do cats get sick? Healthiness is the most important thing anyone that owns a pet should know. Bring your cat to an animal hospital (a vet) for a check-up if your cat is acting weirdly and not-so-catty, such as swallowing small things, throwing up, making weird noises, smells weird or losing fur. Why and how do cats get sick? Because the cats' body is trying to help them fight the germs inside the body that doesn't belong there. Bring your cat to a vet as quick as possible for a checkup, just in case (if your cat starts to show symptoms of sickness), and you could save a life, depending on the situation! Please try not to ——your cat, because it is part of your life... and every living thing on Earth deserves to be treated goodly.

How do we give our kitty a healthy diet, and lower the chances of the kitty being unhealthy again?

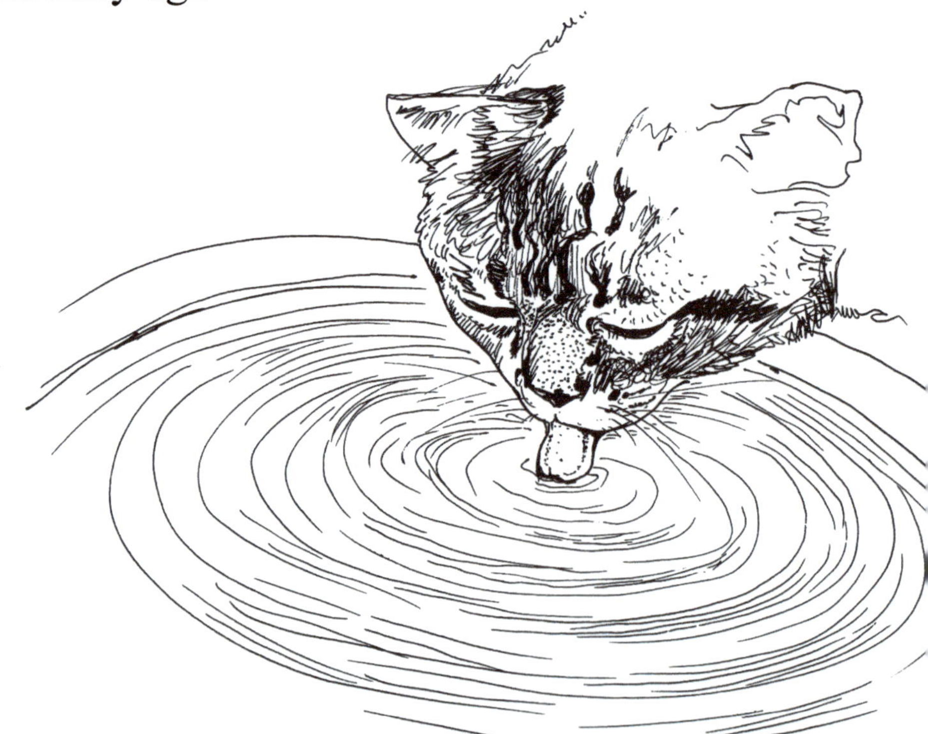

We all love cats, but sometimes we will hurt them accidentally, and without knowing it. How to prepare our cats before the next unfortunate-cat-thingy comes? Food ! So simple, yet so difficult. Now, READ:

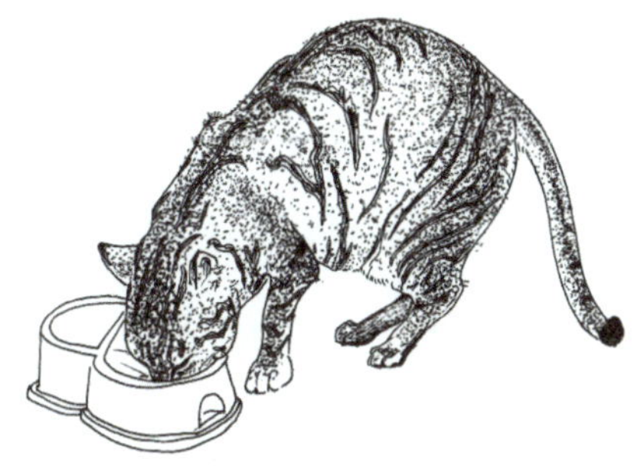

HEALTHY CATS

1.Give your cat its cat food every single day, for 3 meals, but not too much. You don't want your cat to turn into a pig! Never give cats chocolate! Always remember chocolate is like poison to cats!

2. Change the water and cat food the cat

has everyday to make sure the cat always has fresh + germ-free food to eat.

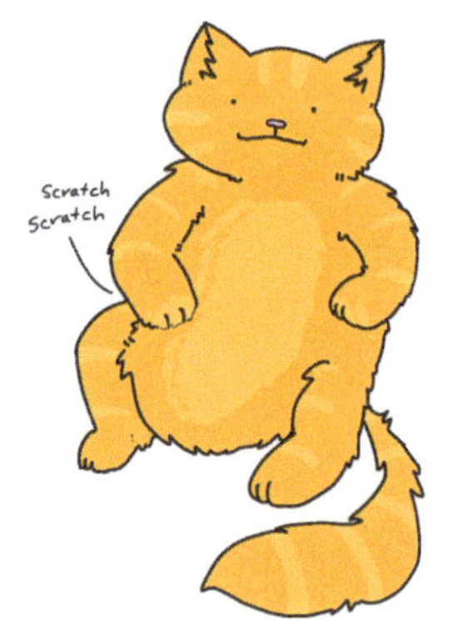

3. Only give your cat its cat food, otherwise your cat might get sick. Only give your cat water and milk, that's the only drink that a cat should drink to stay as healthy as it can be.

4. Only give your cat normal sized cat toys, like the ones that you can buy in a store (because sometimes other additional small toys can be swallowed accidentally by a cat; that would be trouble!)

5. Play and exercise with your cat if you have time so your cat doesn't feel left out or

grow fat

6. Take your cat to the pet hospital if you need to; just to be sure.

7. Follow all the ‘healthy cats’ rules!

Meh looking! Meh also luv u... or else meh going fishy on u!

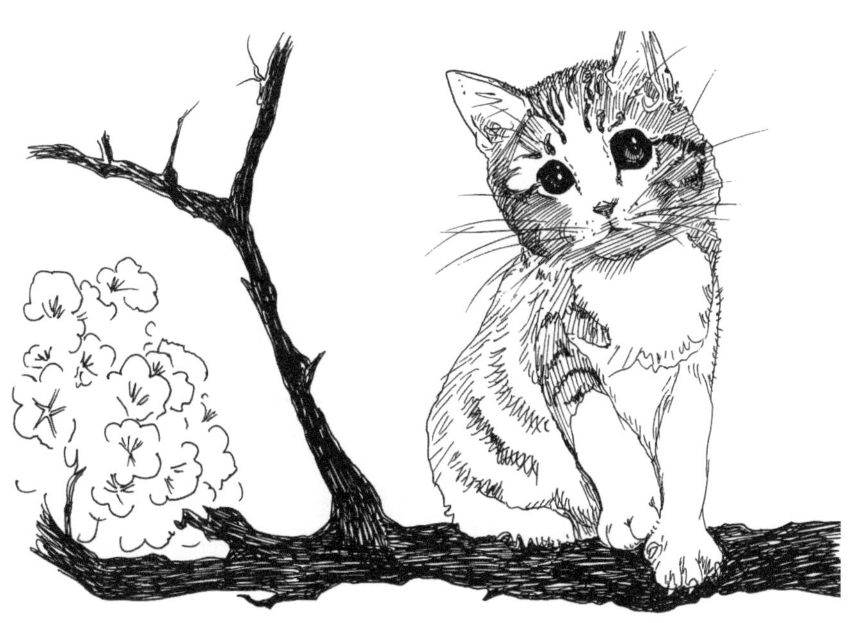

Save Us Cats!

Many owners only care about their own interests, they never even mind their cat's. To them, cats are only pets. They do not deserve what us humans deserve. This is completely serving the opposite of friendship of a cat! Almost all cats you've seen that are happy and healthy is because of the way they are treated. Well... some cats may not be as happy and healthy as the "normal" ones. The truth

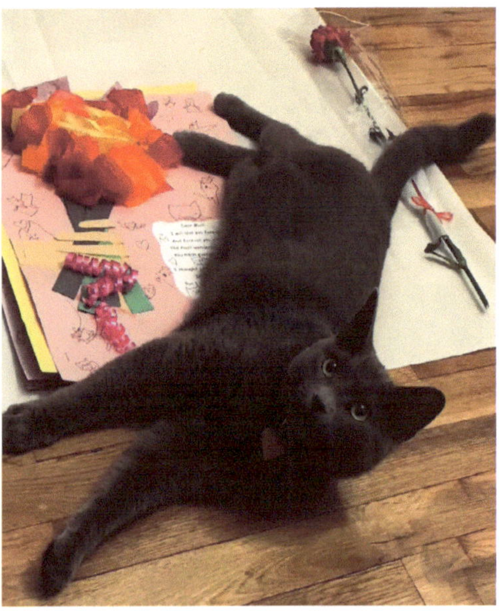

is sad so far... and the cats may not show it. It's up to you to find out. Being happy will make everyone feel better, but being unhappy will have different effects and become a HUGE disaster, too. Sickness, homelessness, afflictions, unhappiness, loneliness, and disabilities could be the end of the world for anything living, that, of course, includes a cat. But what if we are the only ones that could make that change? Make the cat feel more normal and special? A cat's happiness and purpose depends on its owner's actions. Tell you what, this one cat that you adopted is staying with you forever, unless you absolutely have to let it go! Tell ya what, cats have feelings, too! They can feel anger, fear, annoyance, sadness, depression, and even jealousy! Anyways, some of the 'pet owners' never spend time with the cat. The cat may feel forgotten, it's like what we might feel if we were in the same situation. If you see a stray cat in the streets, give it some cat food + shelter and bring it to an animal clinic if you are not adopting it. That is the least we can do. You are your cat's family member, now that your cat is separated from its cat's parents and siblings, so ACT like one. This is why you adopt the cat in the first place; so you feel companionship AND to help a cat. If your cat actually feels like you are a parent to him, he will start "pawing," or step on you

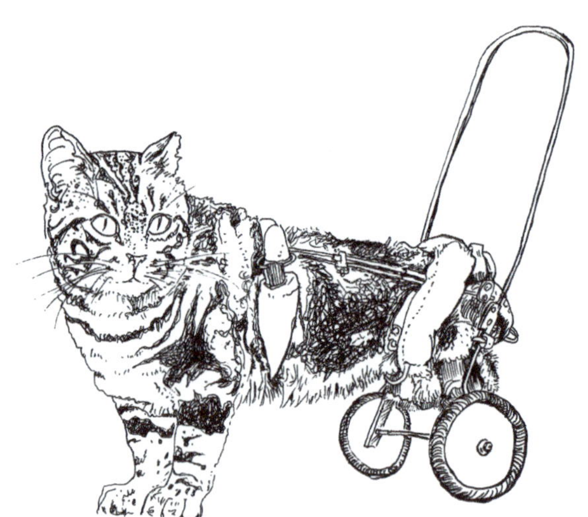

with his paws and sometimes even lick you. Taking the kitten away from its mother is already bad enough; so make the kitten feel less bad (A kitten may be separated from its parents for many reasons; such as it is old

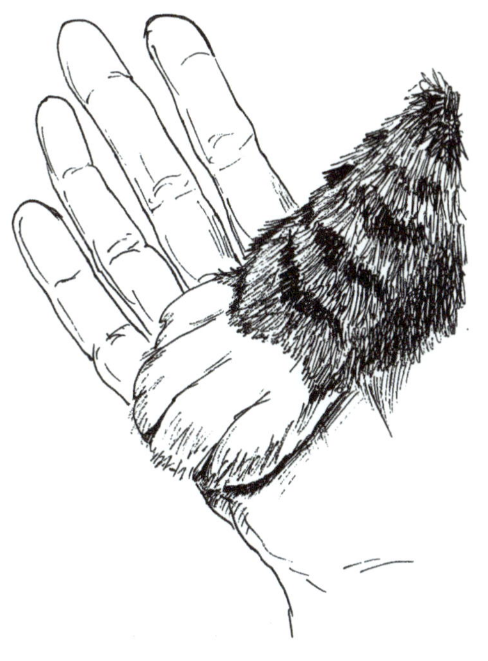

enough to be adopted, the parents died or is gone...). As I was saying, relax, play, and love your cat. Simply: just take more responsibility. We're all sharing the world together, right? You own the cat, then you'll have to take fantastic care of it. If not, why DID you adopt the cat at all? Cats feel every single bit of pain that you might feel if it comes to the same situation, as if it can understand you. Having a cat doesn't mean you would just 'call it cute', instead you should make her/him feel included in the big family. They need you. (Not a toy or a cat tree... but you could adopt more than one cat if you think you are ready and the cat that you already own, as I was saying, feels the same for a cat-relationship.) Anyways, cats were not created for fun, I mean, well, yes, they are troublemakers sometimes too, but mostly, they are for your friendship and what you do for them—sometimes your cat might not show that they like you, and sometimes they even avoid you. That is normal; but if your cat starts defending himself from you and hides, that means you are probably doing something wrong. But you don't have to worry about it; just love and care for the cat as you would do to anyone else and someday soon the cat shall trust you.

HAPPINESS, SAFENESS, AND LOVING IS ALL YOUR CAT WANT AND NEED. Be fair to your creatures, let them believe that they are also part of our world, and everyone is always equal, no matter what they are. (Hey! We came together, so we're leaving together too!)

Small as an ant, big as a whale. (Here we go again... Viva kitty cat... And also-YOU ARE NOT LEAVING MEH!)

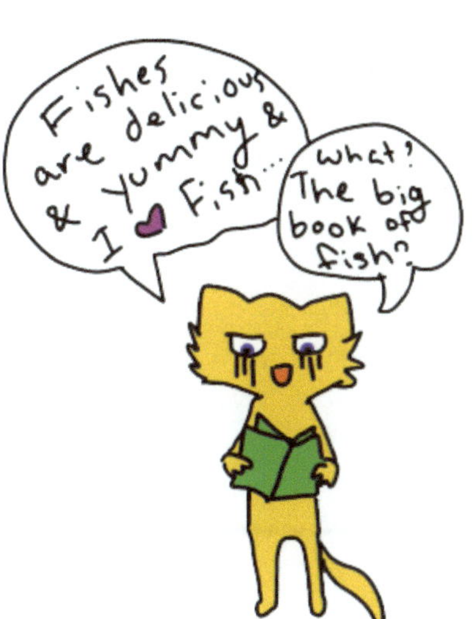

What We Can Do

Caring, loving, "meowing" all around! Make it easier for our poor little cats! Meow!!!

You don't have to adopt a cat, but you should take care of a cat if they need help. I believe you can use all of your heart to take care of a street cat until he/ she is brought to an Animal Clinic. They deserve better.

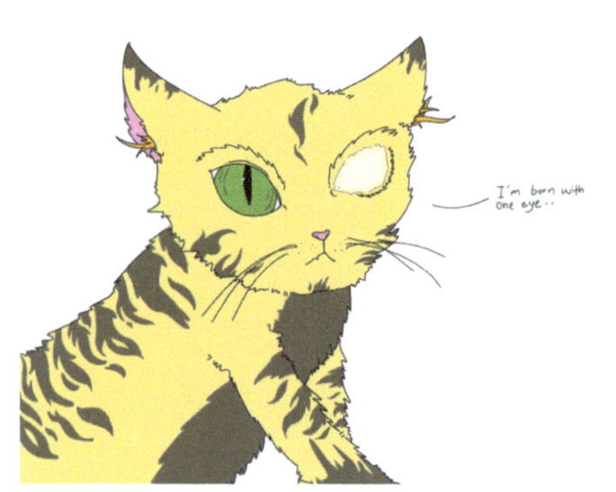

If you want to adopt a cat, think first…! No animals on earth are meant to stay forgotten, they NEED our help-***CATS WOULD NEVER WANT TO STAY IN A PLACE***

WITH NO HAPPINESS nor SAFENESS!

Making the cats happy AND safe, is your biggest job ever after adopting a cat!

Help us cats!!!!!!!!!!
!!!!!!!!!!!!!!!!!!!!!!!!!!!!!!

MEOW!!!!!!!!!!!!!

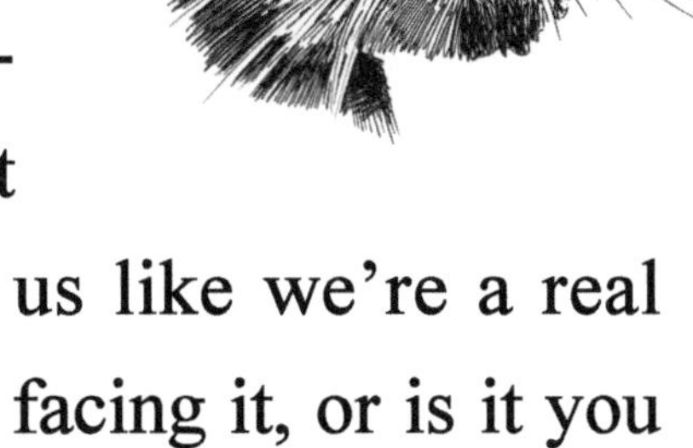

We need freedom, a home, & lovable kitty owners that not just adore us cats, but love us like we're a real cat's meow! Is it the cat facing it, or is it you making it?

SAD True Cats

Cats can be euthanized, or painlessly killed, after staying in a pet store for too long and if nobody adopts them (since more animals are moving in)!

Fishy Word

Euthanasia- painless killing

You may not change your life from getting a cat, but you are going to change the cat's life.

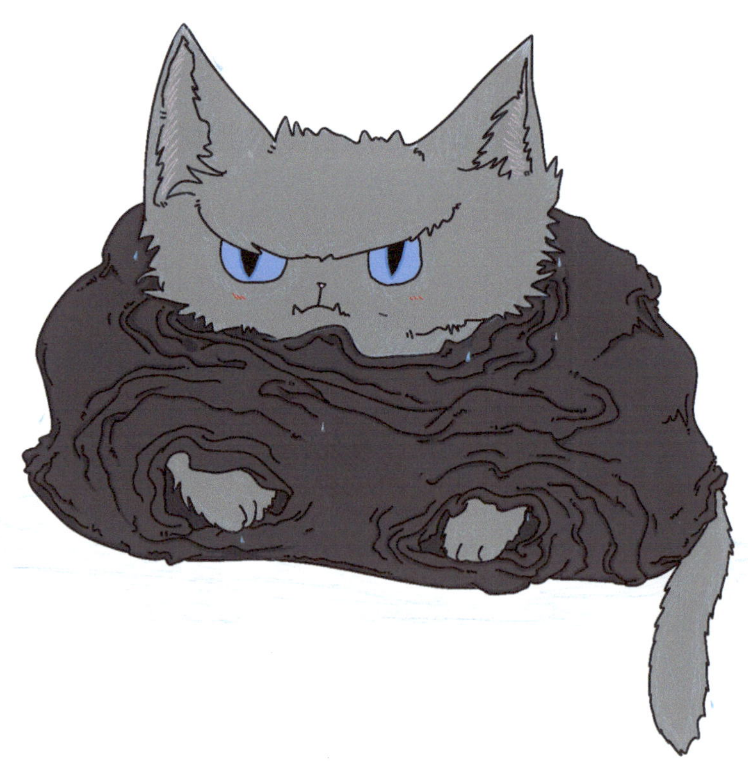

Bath Time!

Bath time! Kitty? KITTY?! Just why won't you like a nice, warm bath?! Well, cats feel uncomfortable when they are wet. Their wet fur makes the cats heavy, cold, and uncomfortable. Have you ever noticed that most outdoor cats don't go out when there's a thunderstorm and hate water a lot? Oh yes, their instincts sometimes matter a lot. Almost ALL cats, big or small, DO NOT like baths, because they HATE to get wet. The cats would prefer giving themselves DIY (do-it-yourself) baths instead of taking DIT (do-it-together) baths with you. Cats lick themselves when they are trying to get cleaned. They would lick themselves not missing an inch, with help

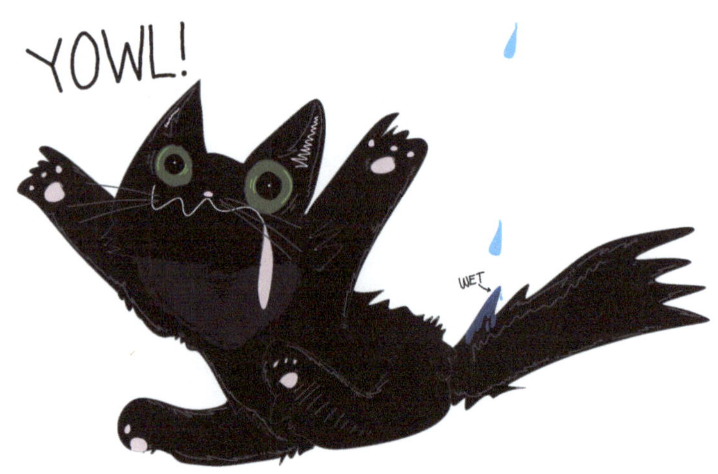

from doing their 'yoga' movements (Cats are one the other world's most flexible animals)! **Cats lick their back fur only when they feel comfortable and safe.** To make sure they're clean enough, the cats have small, soft fur on their tongues. When cleaning themselves, the fur is like fur brushes. If tangled fur comes along, the cat shall use its teeth as hairbrushes to untangle it.

Weirdly True Cat

A cat's body is thinner and smaller than you believe it is. Well, when they are wet. Even a fat, longhair cat can prove you wrong and get you to cancel its next diet. But beware... the hair blower that can make the cat EXPLODE INTO A GIANT CAT FUR BALL! (YES! You heard me right!)

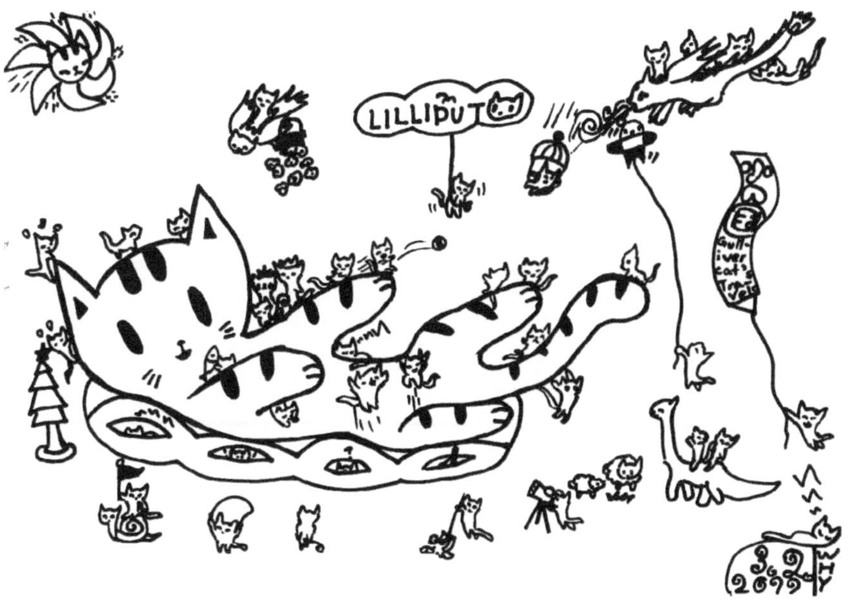

Super Facts!

1. There are at least 50 different kinds of cats, and more are being created and discovered!

2. Cats walk in straight lines and balance really well.

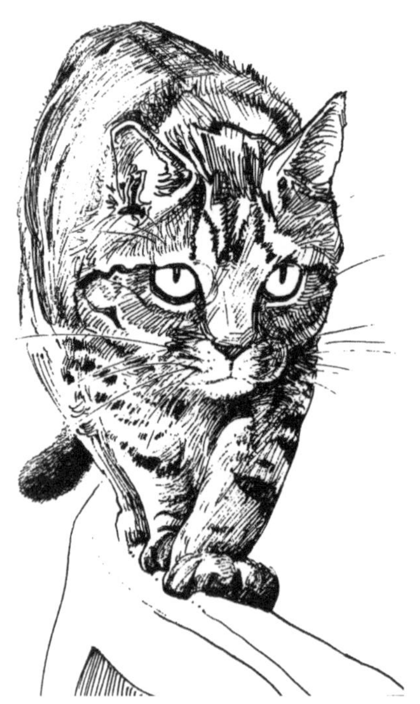

3. Cats are midnight mammals.

4. Cats can go as far as they can; and most of them remember their way home perfectly.

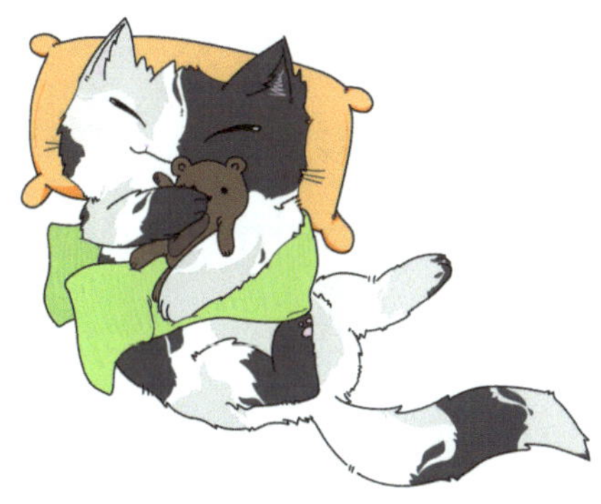

5. Cats are awesome sleepers that can sleep up to eighteen hours each day!

6. When cats are laying down, they'll look like a carpet — especially when there is camouflaging involved. Careful not to sit / step on them!

7. Cats stretch by making EXTREMELY weird yoga-moves.

8. Most cats do not like to share their stuff... so as a result they sometimes GUARD it.

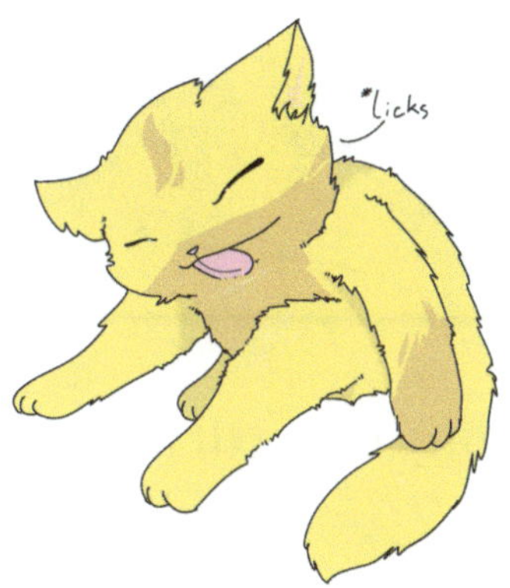

9. Don't make a cat mad 'cause your cat has... deadly claws, tuna breath, powerful legs, sharp eyes, strange ears, moving tail, so BE CAREFUL! Those hard teeth are needed to bite anyone the cat wants to bite on.

10. Cats walk on tiptoes to keep themselves quiet and, well, avoid attracting attention.

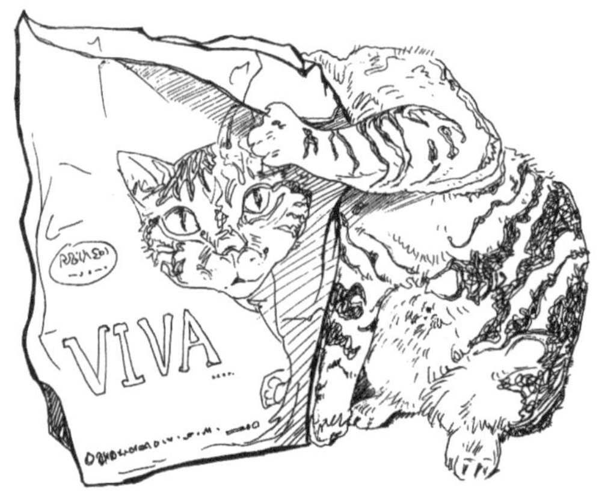

11. Cats play with their tails when they feel like it.

12. Cats' tongues turn into a spoon when they drink water.

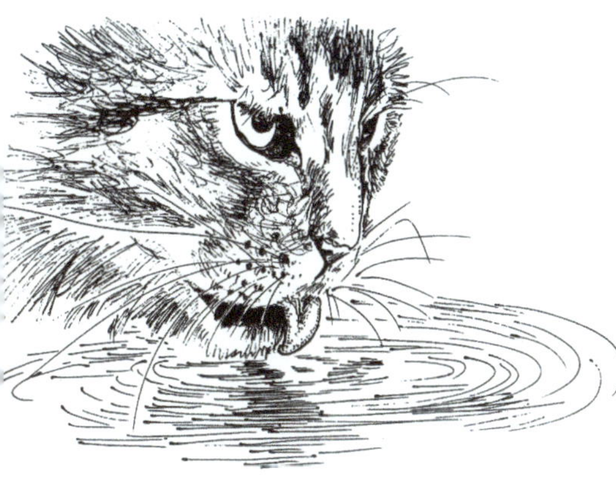

13. Longhair cats—big hairballs; shorthair cats—small hairballs.

14. Cats sometimes eat grass in order to digest hairballs, then they will hack out the hairball along with other wastes (such as food) altogether - - EWWWWW!

15. Cats' whiskers help them "detect" the stuff around them (according to the air flow) and "navigate." Without whiskers, the cat will be bumping here and there.

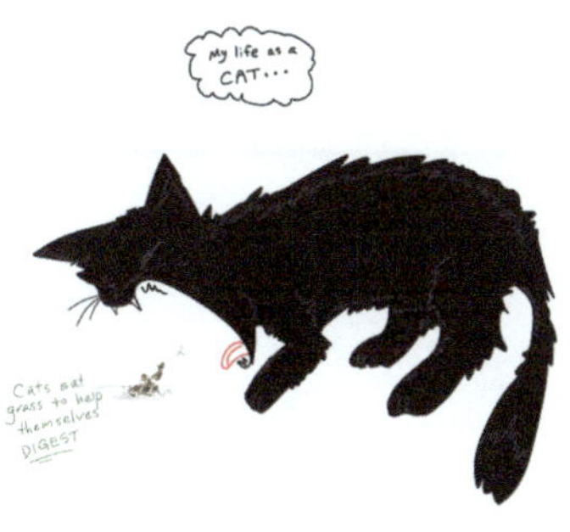

16. Cats can go through thin places and determine whether or

not they can fit, but not before detecting the space with his whiskers.

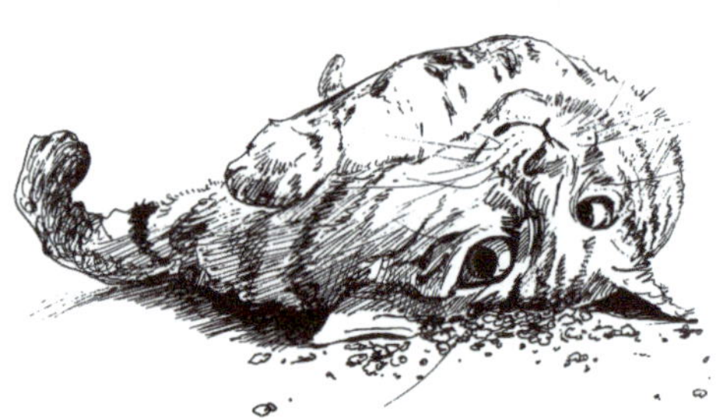

17. Catnips make cats "cuckoo" with enthusiasm for a while... stay out of its way!

18. You know your cat is dreaming if its whiskers twitch or paws move.

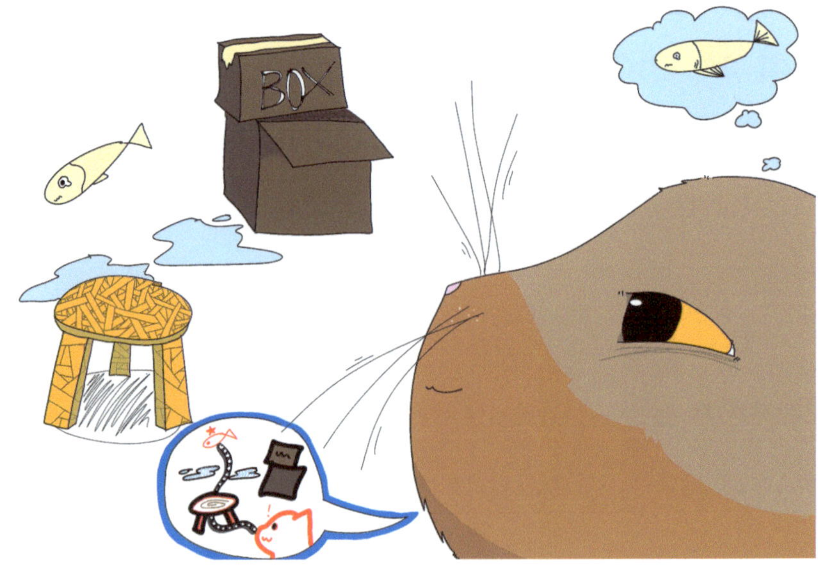

19. Cats can move their ears to hear the quietest sound.

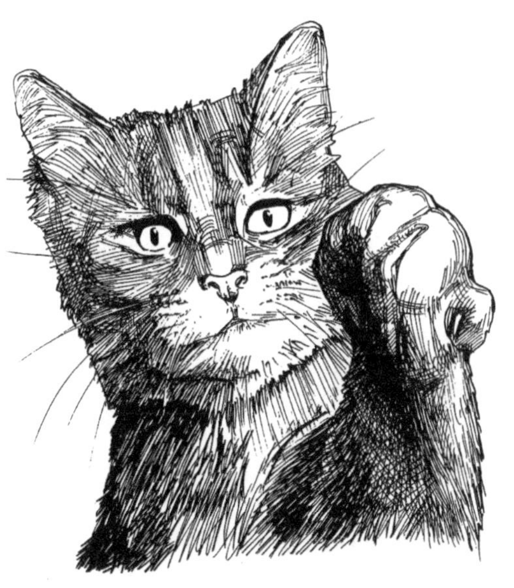

20. Most full-grown white cats with blue eyes are deaf.

21. Most female cats are right-pawed, and male cats are left-pawed.

22. Other words for a cat lover can be called a Ailurophile or a Felinophile. (Tell you what, the author of this book is an Ailurophile!)

23. In Japan, there's an island full of cats called a cat island!

24. Felicette (also known as Astrocat) was the first cat in space, where she stayed for 15 minutes before returning to Earth. (October 18, 1963, sent by Spain)

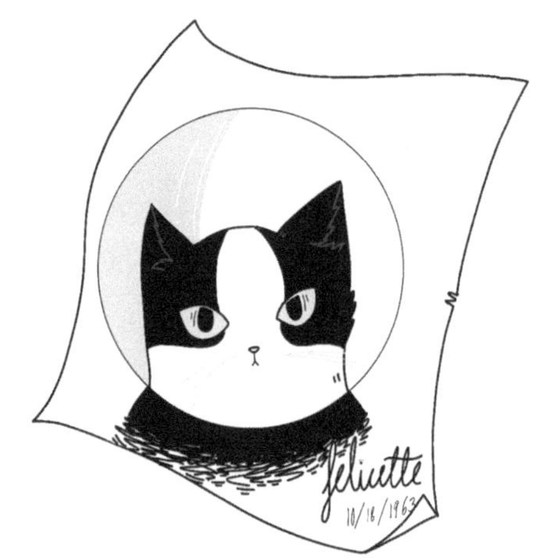

25. Paws, a cat with 28 toes, has 3 extras on each forepaw and 1 extra on each back paw.

26. Even cats have twins, who doesn't?

27. Indoor cats live longer than outdoor cats because their lives have less accidents or sudden movements.

28. Some cats with Guinness World Records are-

I.Tallest (48.4 cm)

II.Shortest (13.34 cm)

III.Longest (123 cm)

IV."Trickiest" (24 total number of tricks)

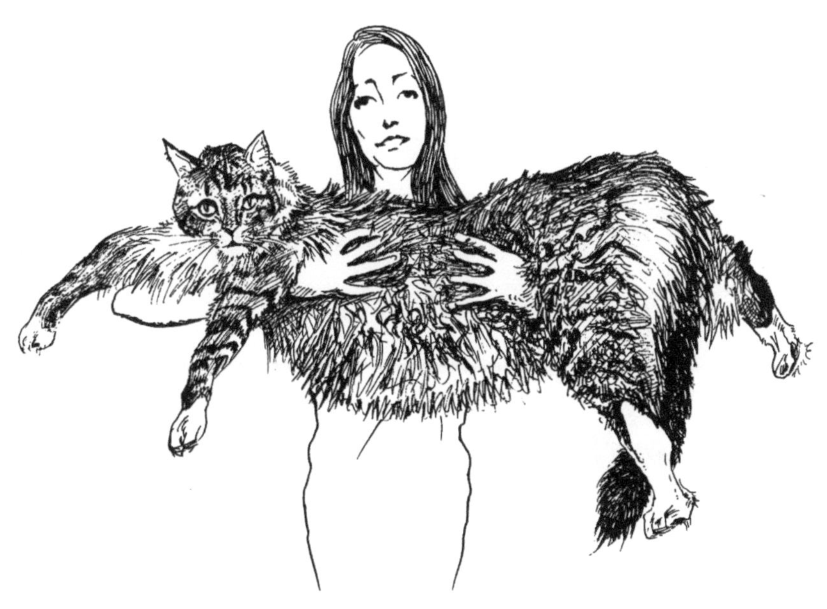

V.Longest purr (17.8 Decibels)

VI.Longest jump (213.36 cm)

VII.Longest tail (44.66 cm / 17.58 in)

VIII.Oldest (38 years and 3 days)

IX.Longest fur (25.68 cm)

X.Newest breed (Selkirk Rex/Aka Poodle cat; Discovery: 2013)

XI.Fattest (11.3 kg)

XII.Largest litter (19 kittens)...

...Earthquake survival cat, longest whiskers......and a lot more!

28. Cats can drink out of the toilet without getting disgusted or sick. (Over here, you can perhaps say that the mother cat is

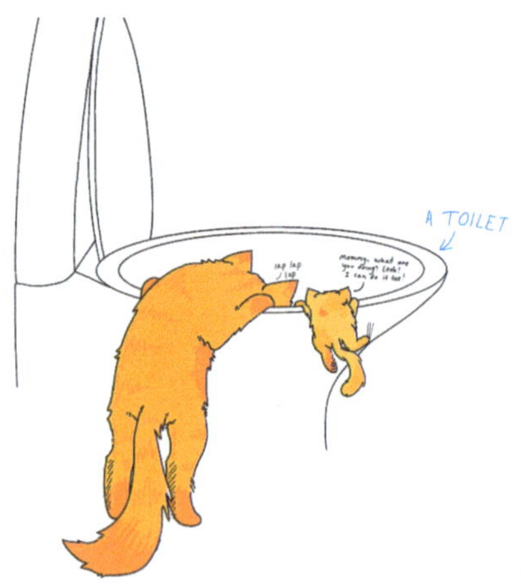

not gonna set a good example...)

29. Cats are the only creatures on Earth that can purr.

30. Chocolate is like poison to cats.

31. Kittens and cats can be trained, these are some simple tricks-

A. High-Paw! Put your hand in front of the cat, and wait until your kitty touches its paw on your hand. High five, and if the kitten gets it after practice and isn't struggling, give it a kitty treat as a reward!

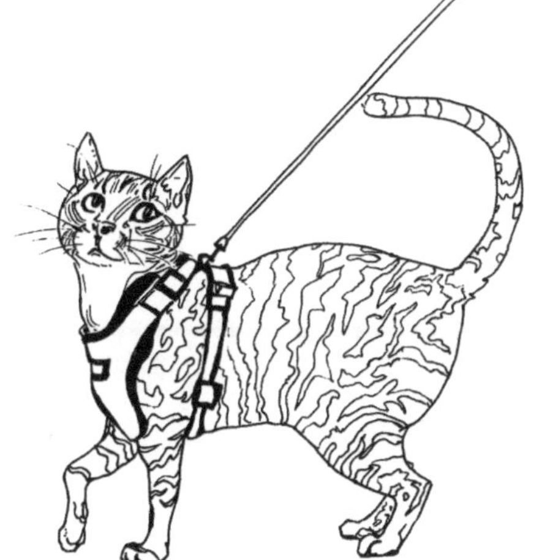

B. Start early! Cats are usually harder to train when they are older than a kitten, so you might as well use a clicker to repeat up to 5 times of practice. (Should only take few minutes or the cat might lose interest) (How to use a clicker; click the clicker button, it will get the cat's attention. Click the clicker again in case the cat loses interest)

C. Walk on a leash! Put your cat on a leash indoors first, walk him around until the cat feels as though it is a normal, easy, harmless thing. You're ready to walk your cat now! (Don't just walk your cat on a normal rope or string, the cat could escape and get lost.)

D. Paw-shakes! Lift one of your cat's paws and shake it softly, repeatedly shaking it until your cat feels less awkward and weird.

E. Carrier training! Getting your cat inside a kitty carrier should be easy for a pet owner. Luring the cat might work, and in order to do that, put something your cat loves (such as a kitty treat) inside. Lift the carrier really easy and soft, and walk around. After some time, your cat should be feeling comfortable being inside a carrier— and there will be no sweat carrying the cat around.

F. Try getting cats into something new! Make the cat get used to the new behavior and lose the old ones. Be straight though, or the cat will be stuck in between and stuff...

32. Cats can't taste sweets... "What does candy taste like?"

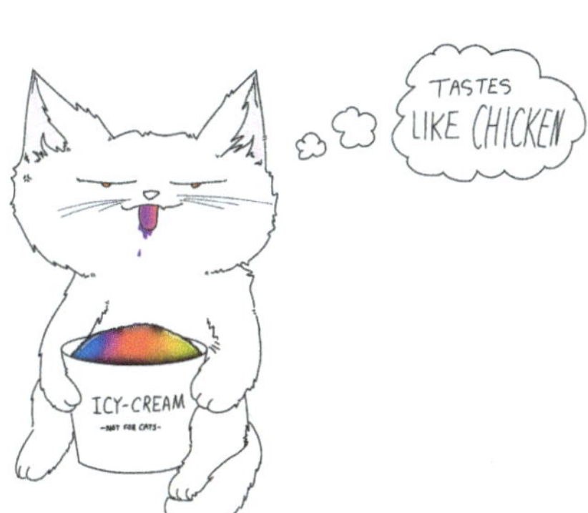

33. Cats have three eyelids... creepy!

34. Cats' eyes are like a mirror—they are truly sensitive (meaning-attached, fast at feeling stuff) to what is happening around.

35. Cats have their very own 'tail language' to tell what they are feeling.

36. Does your pet cat love you enough to take a risk? Some heroic cats help people escape in their sleep, like Boo Boo; howling in the middle of the night, waking up the Morris couple to escape the fire in the kitchen. Instead of running away himself, everyone escaped safely after the cat's warning.

37. **Find my cat!** If your cat is lost, print out papers with information about your cat and distribute it around the neighborhood, so everyone can help look for it. What the paper should include - Name, cat's picture, description, where the cat got lost, reward (if necessary), and phone number.

38. One cat year = full grown in human years!

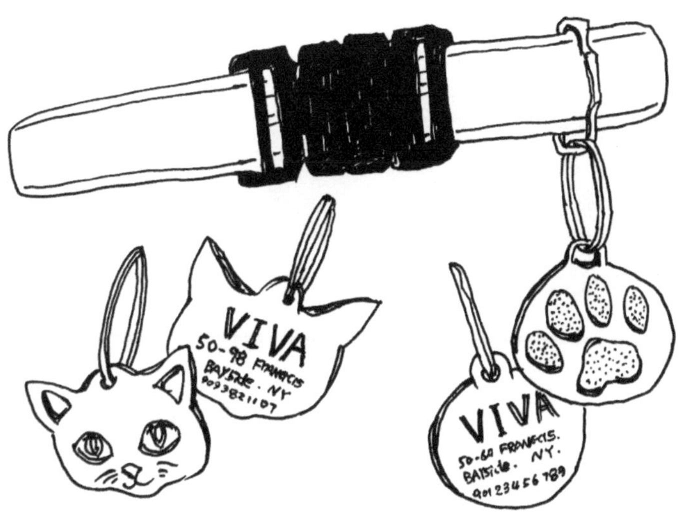

39. Grown cats can have unlimited amounts of litters of kittens... the record is about 360 kittens in a lifetime!

40. Indoor cats usually live longer than outdoor cats because they are well cared for.

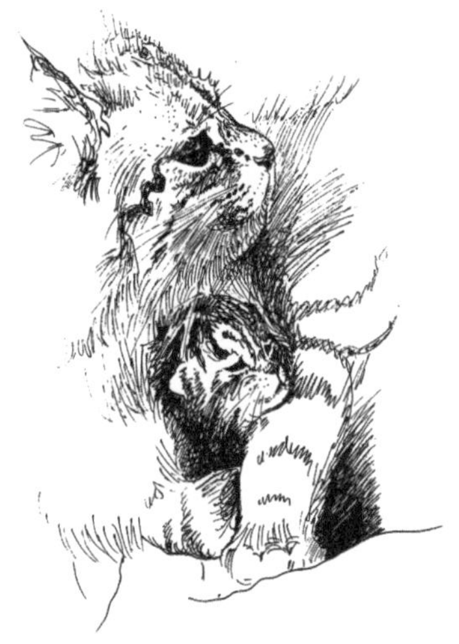

41. Cats spend one-third of their lives doing their 'beauty sleep' and two-fifths of their waking time cleaning.

42. About 2,000 pets can be euthanized (meaning- painless killed) everyday all around the world so that the animal clinics can make room for the new

animals moving in...

43. Cats sometimes make signs like peeing or leaving smells to remember the way back home.

44. Cats have closer DNA to humans than dogs' DNA does.

45. Cats are super sensitive at hearing stuff, you know— they will always have the power!

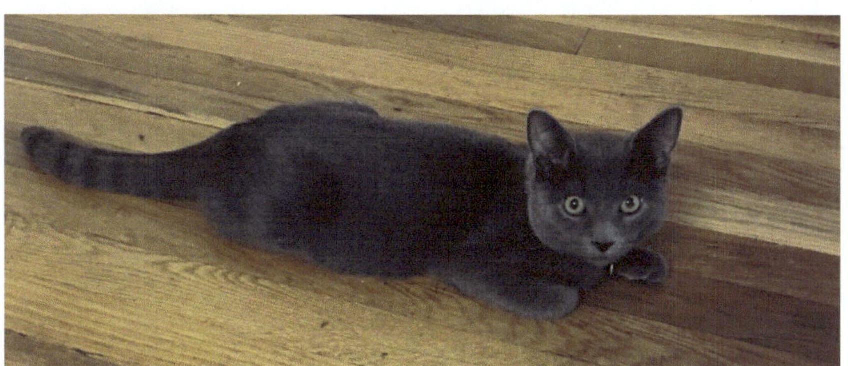

46. Cats' eyesight is 6 times better than humans' eyesight at night.

47. Cats can have a DNA test to see which kind of cat it is.

48. Some cats would "step on milk" whenever they feel comfortable and safe.

49. When a cat gets used to hearing something you say to it, it will get used to it and learn what it means (such as names, or calls like "TIME TO EAT!").

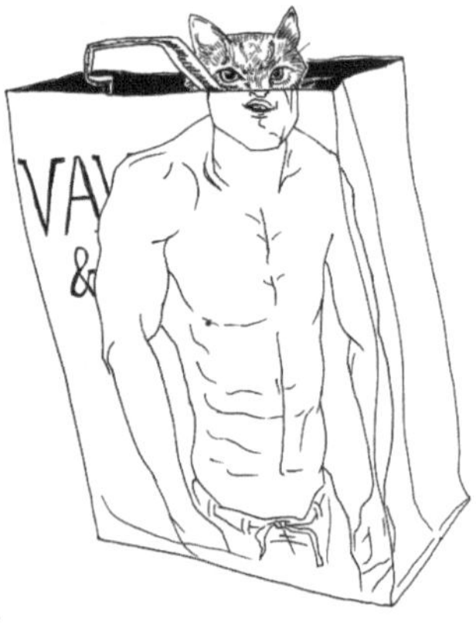

50. Cats can dream... you can tell by looking at their twitching whiskers

while they sleep.

Fishy Stuff

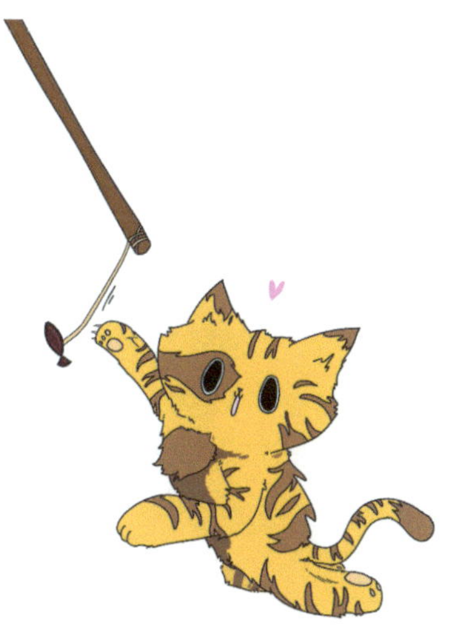

1.Carrier
2.Treats
3.Litter box and scooper
4.Cat tree (optional)
5.Cat toys
6.Scratching post
7.Cat bed
8.Water Bowl
9.Cat Food bowl (Canned/dry food)
10. Collar with phone number and address tag
11. Nail clipper
12. Brush or Comb
13. Paper towels

14. First-aid supplies

15. Feline toothbrush and toothpaste

16. Clipper (optional only used if you want to train the cat; for more information read more :P)

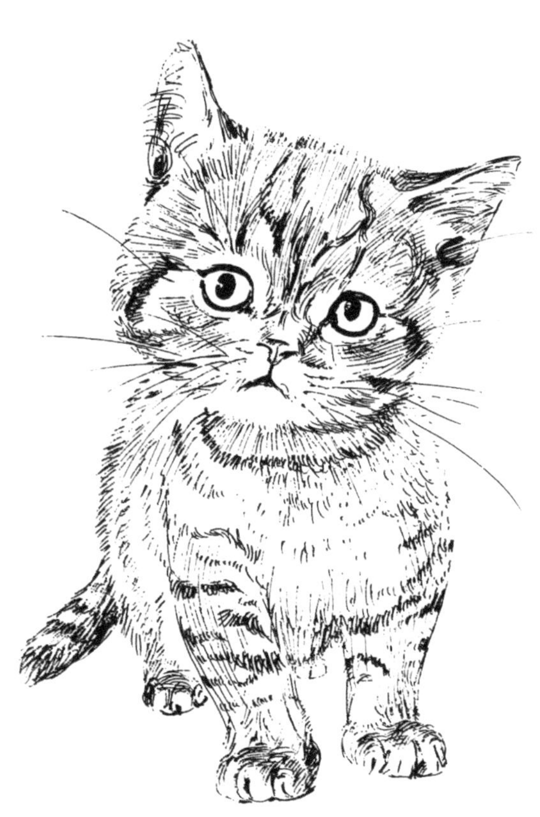

Diet Time, Fat Fellas!

EEEEK!

What a big fat cat!

Ya need a diet! HOW?

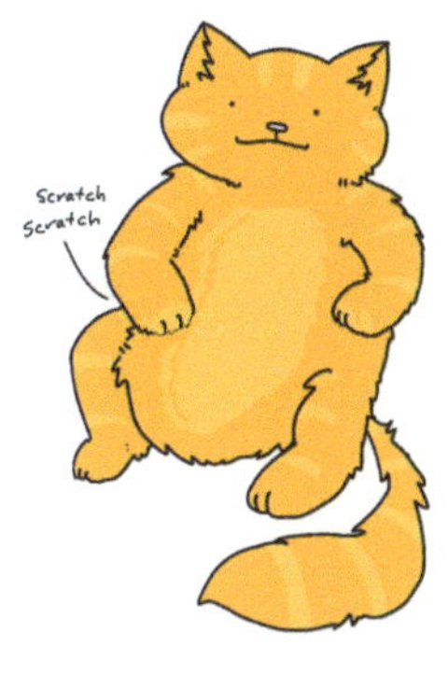

1.Giving less food, more water/milk to your cat.

2.Kitty exercises, remember to use a cat toy and train every second you get (with breaks)!

3.Leave the cat food in a limited amount of time— if he misses it, he's got bad luck!

Never share food with the cat — cats can only eat cat food to stay healthy or they might get diarrhea! (Diarrhea=food poison mixed with POOP!)

Glossary & Index
Cat Words

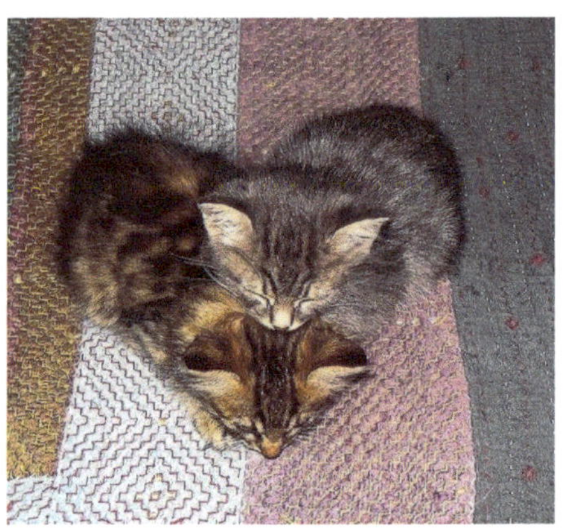

1.***Domestic-*** An animal that stays or lives with and depends on a human.

2.***Felidae-*** The cat family.

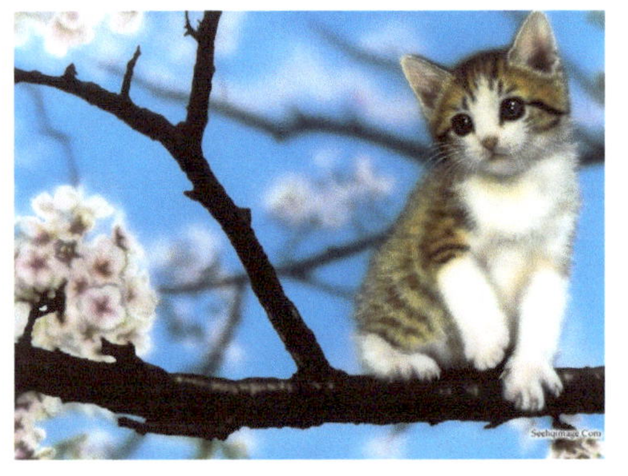

3.***Instinct-*** Behaviors that ALL animals are born knowing how to do.

4.***Litter-*** A group of young born in the same time/litter box-place cats poo poo and pee pee in.

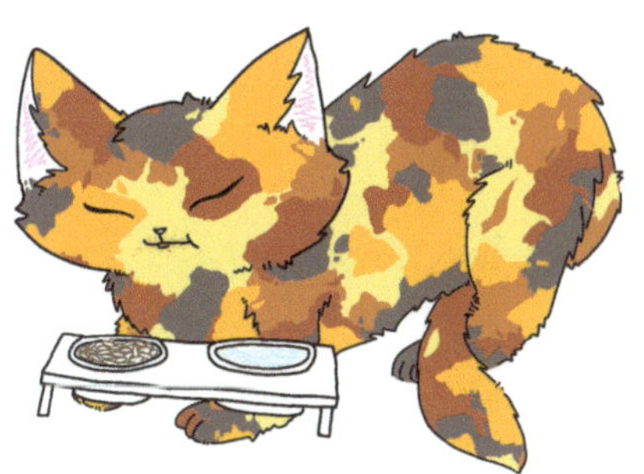

5.***Mammal-*** An animal that drinks its mother's milk (when young), looks like its parents, uses lungs to breathe, and has either fur or hair.

6.***Mouser-*** Cats that help humans catch rodents such as rats.

7.***Prey-*** An animal that gets eaten by another animal.

8.***Vets-*** Doctor for pets.

10. ***Predator-*** An animal that eats another animal.

Index Cats

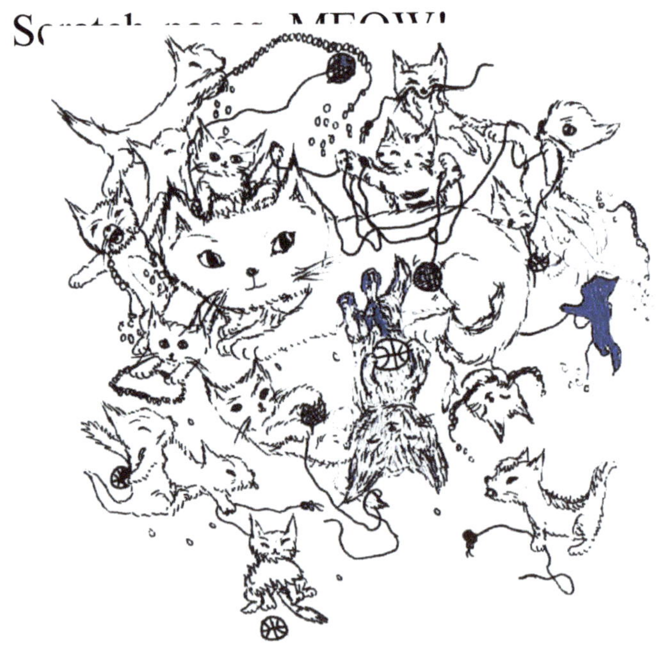

ART

FEEL AND TRY

ART NEVER MAKES SENSE

THAT IS WHY EVERYTHING YOU SEE IS ART

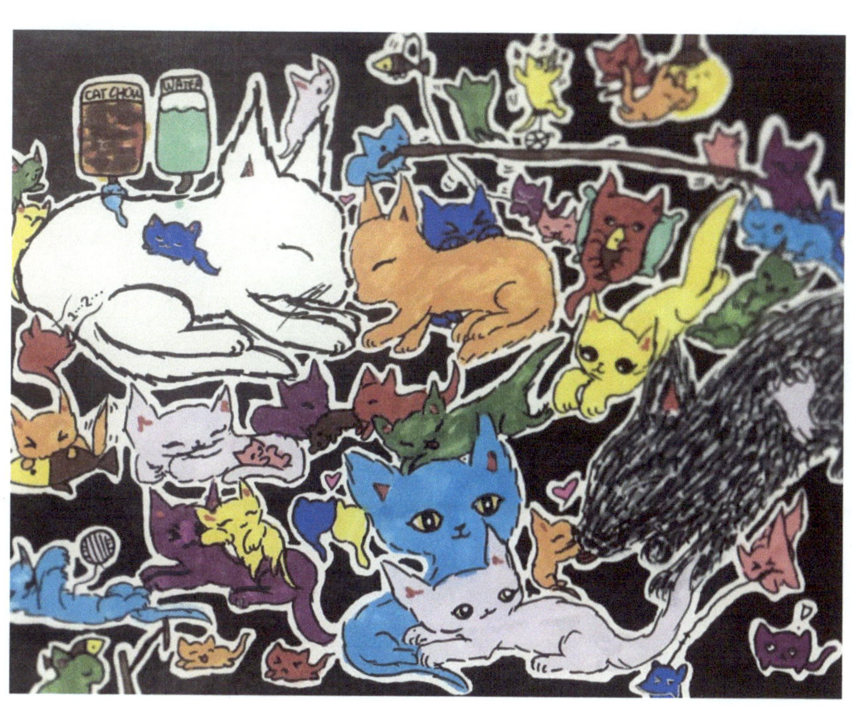

Author Cat Meows

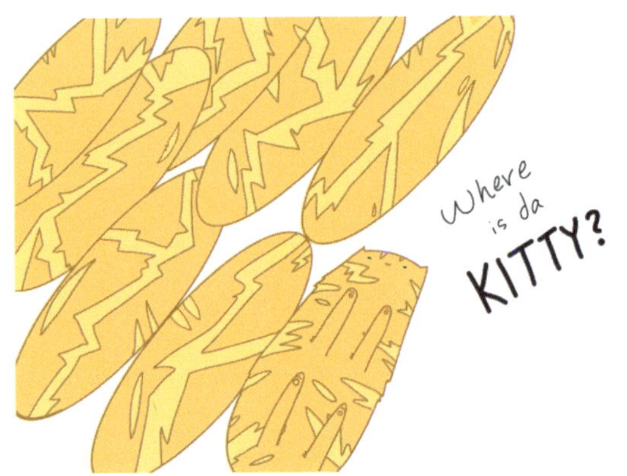

Cat or no cat, they all deserve to be loved. Together, we can help save them all. Now it's your turn... But can you handle everything a cat gives? Is that you facing the consequences, or is the cat facing it for you? After all, it's really nice to have a friend that keeps you company and love.

Don't think this is something small, because one day, it will be YOU facing it...

Book Publisher: Sonia Hu
Book Editors: Phillip Shi, Tyron Shi, Hana Massaiski
Book Designer: Zi Wei Chen

The Power of Cats

出版： 美國龍出版社
Published by Long Publishing Corp.
A New York-based independent publisher
www.ai60.com

ISBN:978-1-953903-03-7

Printed in the United States of America
First Edition: Feb. 2022

www.ingramcontent.com/pod-product-compliance
Lightning Source LLC
LaVergne TN
LVHW070256170826
845679LV00029B/72

* 9 7 8 1 9 5 3 9 0 3 0 3 7 *